GROWING UP ON

David Townsend

OnLine

This book is also available in e-book format from:
www.authorsonline.co.uk

An AuthorsOnLine Book

Published by Authors OnLine Ltd 2002

Printed and bound by Antony Rowe Limited, Eastbourne

ISBN 0-7552-0068-3

Authors OnLine Ltd
15-17 Maidenhead Street
Hertford SG14 1DW
England

Visit us online at www.authorsonline.co.uk

Preface

At the age of fifty-four I was taken seriously ill with CFS, and spent many months in convalescence. Having been almost house bound, off times unable to hold a paper, without my arms aching and needing a lot of rest, I was seeking to find how I could usefully spend my time. Being that my mind had been released from a multitude of responsibilities, at home, with church and work I began to reminisce on the time I spent growing up on our family farm, a mixed farm on the border of Herefordshire and Worcestershire in some of Great Britain's most beautiful countryside.

As the years pass by I am growing more and more to appreciate that the generation my father and I grew up in was a time of great transition. The century that my father was born into saw the decline of horses and the introduction of the tractor. Gang manual labour, which created a great community spirit, was fading with the introduction of mechanisation.

Farming involves a creative mind, strength of character, as well as the ability to improvise, like when machinery breaks down or animals fall ill.

I saw many of these historic experiences being lost, skills that in a day to come may need to be reintroduced for us to survive. So I felt the urge to put pen to paper and relive those years, which young folk today may never have the pleasure to enjoy.

In this book my experiences include the happy and difficult times together with the occasional humorous moments.

My prime motive is to record how it was, to show how basic and simple life was, but although life was hard work, it was very enjoyable and rewarding.

I would like to dedicate this book primarily to my late mother and to John one of our loyal workers who both died during the years 1999 and 2000.

David. F. Townsend. 2002.

Acknowledgements

Many thanks to Simon Hindle for Plate 4:8,
and to Lorna Kyte for Plates 4:2.and 4:3.

Also thanks to my father together with my brothers and sister who
helped to compile the history contained in my book.

Contents

Map of the Farm

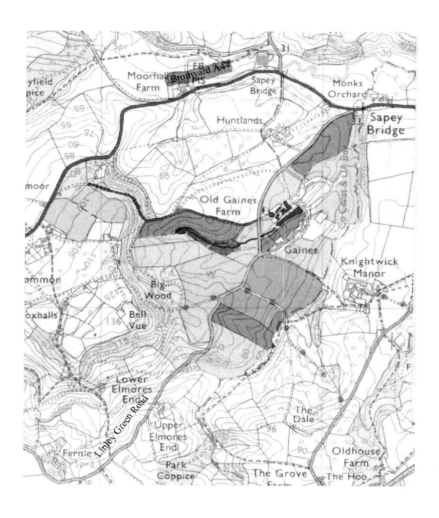

Growing Up On The Farm.

By

David Townsend

Introduction

Up to the mid 1960's there were many medium size mixed farms across the country, until large mechanised farming methods came in, spoiling the community spirit.

For anyone living on a mixed farm, there was always something going on which bonded the community together. Anyone visiting the farm would soon be drawn into the activities on the farm be it collecting the eggs, feeding the chickens, lambs or calves, or helping to drive the sheep and cattle from one field to another. On a warm summer day it was a pleasurable experience to help prepare an afternoon tea and join the family on a picnic in the hay or harvest field, and sit with the workers during their much-needed breaks. On being invited into the farmhouse kitchen you would always be welcomed by the waft of cooking cakes, or bacon frying in the pan, and be asked to stay and partake of whatever was freshly cooked.

The writer covers most aspect of life as it was growing up on a mixed farm, bringing together the good times, with a touch of country humour like fishing in the lake and managing only to catch a chicken, as well as the bad experiences he went through. School life at high school meant a long ten mile bus journey to school and back each day, then come weekends when the cowman had his weekend off meant two long tiring days work, fetching cows in for milking at 6-30am expectedly falling asleep while journeying to chapel three times on a Sunday. In Springtime the author would spend up to sixteen hours a days on the tractor ploughing and tilling the land ready for planting.

For anyone who is thinking of starting the *good life*, or learning some of the old traditional ways of farming this book would be a valuable addition to their bookshelf, as it explains in some detail the methods and techniques used in looking after poultry, rearing animals and growing crops.

Chapter 1

The Early Years

My parent's marriage, starting the farm, and pre-school days.

My father was born the 30th September 1916 in the village of Harewood End adjoining the banks of the river Wye in the beautiful county of Herefordshire. Dad's father, Grandad Townsend was head Wagoner at Bromley Court, a farm in the village run by Aubrey Roberts. When Dad was thirteen, Aubrey Roberts offered Grandad Townsend one of his farms New Mills, to rent, and generously helped him to settle in. Two of my father's brothers Geoffrey and Albert carried on running the farm for some years after grandad retired. Uncle Albert later left the business solely to Uncle Geoffrey, who finally gave up the farm when he retired.

Plate 1:1 Dad on his Motorbike

Dad attended the small school in the adjoining village of Little Dewchurch together with his four brothers and one sister.

After leaving school, he spent his first two years working as a farmhand at a farm in the village of Little Birch, some two miles away from his home with an income of four shillings a week. He then got a job on a farm near Worcester on the banks of the river Teme in the village of Callow End. His prime task was looking after sheep which he enjoyed, although reluctantly he also had to help run the dairy herd. Dad tried to avoid this task whenever he could, as it entailed milking the cows twice a day by hand. When he came to live near Worcester, he joined the local Brethren Chapel in Charles Street, where he met my mother.

My mother was born in New Zealand. Soon after they were married my mother's parents Gran and Grandad Davies had two children a boy and a girl, then emigrated to Invercargill in New Zealand leaving the two children with their in-laws in St. Johns, a suburb on the west of Worcester. During their stay in New Zealand they lost both the children through illness, and while they were abroad, on August 4th 1913 mother was born. Mother kept the loss of her brother and sister a deep secret for most of our adult life eventually sharing her loss with my youngest brother Gordon.

When mum was seven, her parents, possibly due to the loss of their two children decided to return to England, a long six-week journey by sea. My mother suffered severely with seasickness the whole journey and had to be taken straight to hospital on return, to be given help to build her strength up again. My mother told me some years later, that on return they lived in a converted railway carriage, in the Bransford area near Worcester, then staying with relatives in St. Johns, Worcester before buying a house five miles out of town in a hamlet called Doddenham. The house called Devils Leap, sat on the brow of a wooded bowl shaped valley where a tee of roads met in the hollow steep dark dell, with a babbling brook passing through.

Mum first started school at Comer Gardens, in St. Johns, working hard to catch up two years of education, then when the family moved to Doddenham she moved to the school in the neighbouring village of Broadwas, finishing at Knightwick school where she made good progress, which was the neighbouring village to the farm she and my father came to live at when they were married.

2

Mum started her working life in domestic service at an hotel in St. Johns, which has since been demolished near to Canada Way on the Malvern Road.

During this period she also joined the Christian Brethren Chapel in Charles Street, Worcester.

Dad and Mum were married in the Worcester chapel on September 6th 1941 moving to Old Gaines Farm, in the following November. The farm was about 150 acres in all set in the small village of Whitbourne, right on the border with Worcestershire and Herefordshire. As a mixed farm it produced fruit and corn, with breeding beef cattle, pigs, sheep and a few laying chickens. The farm was rented from the Rigley family, a gentry's family who lived in the Gaines Mansion. The front of the farmhouse a black and white oak timbered house with wattle and daub (oak slates inter woven together with lime and horse hair daub) between the beams, sat in an idyllic position opposite the rear of the mansion facing a one-acre lake and a small orchard.

Plate 1:2 Dad and Mum on their wedding day

After a one-week honeymoon with friends at Little Birch near Hereford the first two months of their married life was spent living

3

with mum's parents at Bransford. The rent agreement for the farm did not start till the beginning of November, but the previous occupiers, rather than plant up the land and charge my father for it, allowed Dad to take horses and start to plough and plant corn.

Mum's parents Gran and Grandad Davies soon came to live in the annex of the farmhouse. Dad found Grandad Davies very valuable on the farm. He was a wheelwright by trade able to make ladders anything up to forty rungs high, suitable for the varying sizes of fruit trees in the four orchards, which comprised of a small quantity of plum and damson trees together with pears and a large variety of apples, particular bramley's. The rest of the apples went for cider making.

I was born on October 6th 1945 the eldest of five, four boys and one girl.

My earliest recollection of farm life was standing in the stable yard behind the stable entrance and gazing at the enormous backsides of these great carthorses. Although this is the only recollection of seeing them, apparently I must have favoured one called Captain, who in my young child like vocabulary called Gee-Gee-Cat-Bang. For many years after, there was much evidence of harness and horse drawn machinery around to help keep the memories. In particular was a two wheeled cart which would have been used for general haulage, and lay for many years gradually rotting next to the Dutch barn. There was also a dray built by Grandad Davies that had its shafts converted for towing behind the tractor.

During my mother's childhood stay at Devil's Leap, Grandad Davies needed to clean the well out. Mum was very fearful of grandad carrying this out, having experienced the dramatic sea journey from New Zealand to England. This fear of water seemed to continue into later life, because dad had to put a 6 ft high fence around the front side of the farmhouse to prevent my brother Paul and myself getting near the lake, only 3o feet from the front door. Once my brother Paul and I reached our early teens Dad kitted us both with a fishing rod and allied equipment. Rising at dusk, we would head for the manure heap and fork out a few juicy worms, or pinch some bread crusts from mum's bread bin to make bread paste. We then spent a good deal of our time at the lake side, catching and fighting the carp who were very skilled at finding the nearest water reeds, or the occasional eel which seemed to have a

4

way of gluing themselves to the bed of the lake, and then once out of the water nearly always discovered it had managed to completely swallow the hook. It is alleged that my youngest brother Gordon once managed to hook one of the laying hens. Impossible, you may say. He, having rebated his hook with bread paste, then having adjusted the line length at the end of his rod, drew the rod over his right shoulder to cast out .He suddenly felt a sharp tug as one of the hens saw the opportune meal coming her way, giving a quick peck got true and firmly hooked. I have never discovered what transpired to part hen from hook, but nothing untoward seems to have happened to the hen.

I recall a missionary friend from India called Jim staying with us. He decided it would be a good idea to catch one of these fish, cook it on an opened fire and have a meal from it. It all went to plan until the point of cutting the fish up to eat. Due to the farm being so close to the lake, it was convenient for one of the drains from the kitchen, which would have had some seepage from the farmyard, to feed into the lake. We also discovered that where this drain entered the lake it was a favourite feeding area for the fish, and so there was some jostling by fishermen for a pitch at this point, at the expense of coping with the odours, especially on a hot summer's day. As soon as we started to dissect the fish all the odours from the drainage rose with the steam from the fish. The fish was rapidly discarded, and fishing from the lake for a meal was never tried again.

During the time I was in the local junior school at Whitbourne, I discovered from some of the other lads how to make a catapult. I constructed one out from an ash cutting into a vee shaped twig. I then got a piece of leather from a disguarded shoelace from one of dads old boots and some cotton material two inches square, taken from some of the off cuts that mum used to make her rag rugs with, put two slits in the clothe, threaded the leather shoelace through and tying the two ends to a piece of elastic onto the vee stick.

At the top of our farm drive was a duck pond, and in the spring you would regularly see eggs that had fallen out of a nest belonging to one of the ducks or moorhens. The ducks belonged to John and May Hindle who worked on the farm, and lived in one of the farm bungalows behind the pond.

As I wandered up the farmyard to the pond with my catapult in one hand, I picked up some of the stones from the yard, considering the eggs to be ideal targets. Due to lack of practice my only way of getting a bull's eye meant I had to stand close to the edge of the pond, near to the eggs lying in the weeds on the edge of the pond. I took aim pulled the elastic to full measure let the stone fly with a 'splash' as the shell collapsed and the contents rebounded up like an explosion splashing all over my jacket and trousers. I did not realise till then that eggs that are good sink, but once they begin to ferment, gases build up inside, and then float to the surface. This was a rotten egg, and the worst part was the smell, which is a very obnoxious and gassy smell. Sheepishly returning to the farmhouse, my presence was quickly recognised, and mum knew what the smell was and who was giving the show away. No more shooting practise with floating eggs.

During the school holidays, before Paul and I were old enough to start school, Dad would frequently take us to the Thursday market day in the local town of Bromyard. If he wanted to buy some one-day-old calves to suckle on a freshly calved cow, or take some weaned pigs to the market he would load them in his little two wheeled high-sided trailer, and tow them behind his Morris 12 car. If he was taking pigs to market or any vetenery work was to be done on the farm, especially killing one for the farmhouse, I had to be taken care of, because the sound of pigs squealing would gravely and emotionally upset me. So whenever the pigs were being seen to, Mum would cart me off or wait for school days to ease my anxiety before carrying out such work. It was pleasurable walking through the market stalls when I could not hear the pigs being persuaded into their pens. It was a pleasure seeing all the locals, both farmers and smallholders meeting to sell their home grown wares. We would often overtake a horse and trap on their way to market. Walking through between the stalls of fresh eggs vegetables and jars of homemade jam making my way towards the main cattle market I noticing some freshly plucked hens hanging up for sale, with a hand written notice saying 'Boiling chickens for sale'. I just wonder how many folk fell for that advert, as this indicated these hens were too old and tough to roast, and needed boiling rather than roasting in order to tenderise the meat.

On entering the main gate of the market as I walked the corridors down between the animal pens, I was fascinated

6

watching the farmers prodding the calves with their drovers sticks, so that the animal would turn round so the farmer or dealer could have a good look at, or then dig their fingers into the backbones or hind rump of the lambs to assess how much meat they were carrying.

The auctioneers had their own team of workers. There were the drovers who met the farmers at the market entrance to direct the animals to the appropriate pens, using their unpredictable sticks, dancing up and down waving there sticks in the air as if they were on a trampoline, shouting *go-on, go-on.shu..shu*..followed by loud shrill whistles to create fear and to aid the animals on. Close behind in the cattle pens, were men with a glue brush and a pack of three-inch diameter, numbered paper discs, splashing glue on the rump of each animal, and then slapping a disc on for identification.

Getting to the market early was crucial, because it dictated how long you'd have to wait for your animals to be sold. Once we had been round the pens to assess the competition it is time to get a place in the selling ring. You would have no doubt as to if the sale was starting, for one of the drovers would start pealing a large bell for a few moments and then you would hear the auctioneer start the bidding in a distinctly loud voice. You had to bustle your way through and up the different levels of platforms till you could get a good view of the sale ring. It is a hive of activity, with one of the drovers ushering the animals round and round the ring, while the auctioneer would be calling out bids in almost indecipherable words in rapid reputation "*at 25 pound, at 25,at 25 who'll give me 30, at 25 pounds*", like the sound of the wheels of a train speeding over the rolling stock. You had a job to know who was bidding. You dare not scratch your nose or make a marked movement with your head for fear of telling the auctioneer you were bidding. Someone would be nodding his head, or lifting a sale programme or stick, or just a glancing eye at the auctioneer, then a loud clunk as the auctioneer would bring his gavel or stick on to the podium followed by a sharp word "*Sold*!". There would be a moment's pause, except for the din of clanging gates opening and shutting, and the beat of sticks and shouting as the drovers continued to drive one lot of animals out and the next lot of animals for entry into the ring. Once the cattle were sold the auctioneer would move out into the main market, legging himself up onto a length of builders planks, which were sitting on the side of the pens. To minimise the handling, all the sheep and pigs were sold in their pens.

Paul and I would find the auctioneers selling skills fascinating, so we would get our wellies on when we got home, saunter up to the top cattle yard, and while I with a stick, would march the cattle round the yard, Paul sat on the gate and auctioned them. Some of Dad's cattle had been sold many times unbeknown to him.

Plate 1:3 Dad's first car

Chapter 2

Feeding the animals

Cows, calves, pigs and poultry.

When living on a farm there is no need for an alarm clock. Jack Burraston one of our farm workers would arrive on his bike, having travelled two miles from the nearby hamlet of Bringsty Common. In the summer the cattle needed much less feeding, for the cows with their calves could go out to the pasture and graze. But in the winter months much time was spent morning and late afternoon preparing and distributing the food for feeding the stock (animals) with the added chore of mucking out the pigs and giving all the animals a layer of loose wheat straw on the floor for warm bedding. When Jack arrived first thing around 7-30am in the morning, you would hear the corn grinder rattle into life. The corn grinder would produce a high-pitched sound as the rough shaped metal drums grated against one another. Then the tune would change to a gentle hum as the corn started to feed into the grinder. The mangolds would be carted and tipped onto the barn floor next to the beet cutter from where they had been winter stored. They were either stored in a heap called a clamp out in the field where they had grown, or in the rickyard covered by loose hay and a layer of soil to protect them from the frost. Once the beet was forked into the feeder hopper, the beet cutter would carry the mangolds along the top of two close running horizontal drums with angular metal teeth to clean the loose soil off and then cut the mangolds into 4 inch slices much like a larger runner bean slicer. Both the corn grinder and the beet cutter were belt driven connected to a pulley on a large shaft running across the upper storey of the bottom barn, driven by an electric motor in the engine house next door. Because of the power surge to start, the switchgear was started in two stages, first at a slow speed in low phase. Then once the machinery was in motion you switched up to full power.

In one corner of the barn were large sacks filled with dried sugar beet pulp, and between the two machines was a clean open concrete space for mixing the food.

One day in my innocence I thought to myself, if this pulp was the residue of extracted sugar, why not chew a little, perhaps it will still yield a little of the sugary taste. So in went a few morsels. As I chewed, it gave a bland, but pleasant taste, but I detected no sugar spitting out the remnants outside the barn door. Not too long after I began to detect a stinging sensation in my mouth, a soreness that stayed with me for some hours. I did not try tasting sugar beet pulp or slices of mangolds again as I found they both had the same effect.

Sugar Beet was one of our saleable crops, so on each occasion that we took a lorry load to the processing factory at Kidderminster, we had the option either to buy back dried pulp in sacks, or have the raw damp pulp delivered loose in the lorry bed. Sugar beet once lifted, had to be loaded by hand in the field, then was tipped onto the edge of the farm driveway, to make easy access to load by hand onto the lorry. The lorry had standard height sideboards, but had a second set of boards hinged on the top to get a worthwhile load. On the side where the loading took place both sets of sideboards would first be lowered, with two workers using special beet forks to load. As the bed of the lorry started to fill the lower set of sideboards would be repositioned, until that part was full then the second set would be put in position. Both farm trailers would remain loaded and be drawn along the opposite side of the lorry, making it easy to load the last few inches of topping up because throwing the last few roots over the six foot high sides from the ground was hard work.

As the beet got up level with the sides you would go round the edge of the lorry wedging the narrow end of the beet in a neat row around the top of the top sideboards to extend the edge of the load slightly, allowing a few more roots to be loaded safely. Harvesting of Sugar Beet was carried out from November to the beginning of February dictated by the length of time the factory processing plant was open. Lifting the beet in very wet weather was difficult, with having to use two tractors at times to tow the three-ton trailer out of the deeply rutted field. Likewise it was difficult to lift the beet in a wet season without some mud left on. When each lorry load arrived at the factory, having gone over the weighbridge, they would have to queue in readiness to reverse onto a ramp. The beet had to be unloaded single handed, so the ramp would tip the lorry a little so as the beet would slide off the lorry to make life a little easier for the driver when unloading. First a sample of the beet would be processed to determine how much weight of soil was on the beet, and then the tare weight of the load would be adjusted accordingly. Farmers knowing that the soil volume would be checked would keep to one side cleaner drier beet to top up the load so that the sample taken at the beet factory would show a better sample, in order to get a better deal for the load.

Whenever Dad decided that we needed a load of fresh sugar beet pulp I would look forward to the lorries late afternoon return. The freshly processed pulp would be conveyed steaming hot into the lorry bed. On arrival the lorry would draw along side the home made concrete bunker, next to the Dutch barn, while I was hastily dressing up to keep out the winter cold and offer some help, being the pulp was so light to handle. I would wear my wellies keeping the legs of my boiler suit on the outside, to prevent the wellingtons filling up with the curly feathery wet grey strips of beet pulp. It was shear bliss trudging around ankle deep in the moist spongy pulp that gave a warm glow to the feet and a moist sweet steamy smell. After a few days the top layer would dry out and change to a brown hard crust with a matt of yellow fungus growing on the top, making it a very attractive feature. Once cool the pulp could then be fed neat to the cattle.

If we decided to feed the animals with the dried beet pulp, it first needed to be moistened otherwise the animals would choke. A quarter of a sack of pulp was placed on the barn floor, with half a bucket of water added in a space in the centre of the pile parted with the shovel. A portion of bran (the outer shell of wheat) together with a shovel or two of pulped mangolds were added and generously mixed together.

You knew when feeding time was imminent, for Jack could be heard whistling a tune, as he mixed the food to the sound of the shovel sliding across the barn floor. A few moments later the latch on the barn front door would drop open and Jack would emerge carrying a large galvanised steel food bin on his shoulder. Moments later, you would hear the wooden yard gate squeak open, followed by a few choice words to the cattle, ' get back...get-back' as the animals heads jostled and bustled towards the food tin on Jack's shoulder eager to get their first mouthful. After a few drum like bangs on the side of the trough to aid the last morsels of food out of the tin, and a squeal of the gate being re-shut, it was back to the barn for another refill.

During extreme winter conditions the cattle would be kept in, so besides being fed with the ground corn, mangolds and sugar beet pulp mixture they needed hay, bedding straw and an ample supply of water. Jack could not drive the tractors, so he had to fetch the bales from the rick yard by hand. Balancing precariously on a barrow he could perhaps carry three to four bales at a time, but it was slow work. Each cow could eat up to half a bale of hay a day. Most straw was used for bedding, but in the depths of winter you would often supplement hay with oat straw, as it was the only straw with any nutrients in it, helping to keep the animals' stomachs full. Both the large enclosed cattle yards had tanks of water with an automatic ball cock to keep them full, but the smaller enclosed sheds, commonly referred to as loose boxes needed water carrying to them. Cows can drink up to ten gallons each day, so this meant a lot of buckets of water when you could only carry six to seven gallons at a time. Each of the loose boxes could house two cows, each having a ten-gallon triangular trough made out of solid concrete. The cows would draw the water up at great speed emptying the trough in moments, requiring two or three journeys before they were finished and you could fill it up. Occasionally one of the animals would have stood with her rear over the trough either urinating or leaving their droppings in it, so you would have to get your hand in with some tufts of straw to clean it out.

Once their thirst is satisfied then all the animal yards and sheds would need bedding down with wheat or barley straw, which could take up to twenty bales and quite some time to shake up and spread out.

First thing in the morning, once Jack started to make a noise with the click of the gate latches, and as he dragged the wooden gates open across the cobbled yard, the animals would soon let you know they were hungry. The cows and calves all start mooing and bellowing, with the pigs giving out impatient squeals and grunts. In addition to the herds of beef cattle

Apart from the hard wintertime the cows would run out in the fields with the Hereford Bull. Morning and evening the cows including the bull would be brought into the cowshed and tied up.

Plate 2:1 Willy and Betty Price

Then the calves that were kept in a shed attached to the cow shed would be let into the cows to suckle. Some hustle and bustle would take place as the calves jostled to get to the cows to suck, with you having to grab the calves around the neck to redirect and to discipline the bustling calves to make sure an equal number of calves went to each cow. After some training one or two of the cows would have been, and now through habit, be ushered into one of the four loose boxes near to the farmhouse. The loose boxes were utilised as a place to isolate animals that were sick or imminently due to calve as well as an extra cowshed. One of the cows would have had some of her milk taken off by hand milking for the farmhouse. Jack would position himself on the stool, by the side of the cow's udder, placing the bucket, pitched forward, between his legs, with the base resting on his feet. Then with his cap pitched sideways and with his head dug forward into the front of the cows thigh, he would settle down to start milking. You needed your cap well forward and to the side to prevent the wet juicy tail from lashing your face, to keep the flies away, and give Jack an early warning and inhibit the cow from lifting her foot and kicking the bucket. Once seated Jack took a teat in each hand, alternately squirting the milk into the empty galvanised steel

13

bucket. As the first 'squirt- squirts' shot into the empty metal bucket it gave out a tinny musical ring, then changed to a dull tone as the bucket began to fill. From the loose box next door to where the cows were tied up, a further group of calves would be let out to feed on the cows. When the calves had drawn all the milk from the cow's udder the calves would start to give the udder a good duff with their nose, to encourage the cow to let more milk down. It was time to usher the calves back to their own loose box again.

Dad often told the story of the young lad experiencing his first day on a farm. This lad knew nothing about farming or country life. The farmer standing outside his farmhouse door called for the lad, and presented him with the traditional wooden three-legged stool, a metal milking bucket and sent him off without instructions into the cowshed to milk the cow.

A short time later the farmer could hear noises coming from the cowshed. He could hear the feet of the cow slipping on the hard stone floor, together with the metallic sound of the bucket being given some rough treatment, not to mention what type of language the lad was giving the cow for not co-operating. Some moments later the lad emerged with the bucket crumpled almost flat and the stool with its legs missing. Seeing the lad emerging from the shed looking somewhat distressed, the farmer hastily emerged from the farmhouse greeting the lad with *"What's the matter son?"*. *" Sir,"* he responded, *"I could not get the cow to sit on the stool."*

Due to the lack of suitable medication, little could be done if calves get pneumonia, but I remember dad getting a sack, pasting it with diluted mustard, wrapping the sack round the calves body to increase its body temperature, to draw the infection out. He then would take two or three fresh eggs, break them into a dish and whip them till the yoke and white were well mixed. Dad would mix up the raw eggs with milk, and with the aid of a sheep-drenching gun, down the side of the jaw, gently trickle it down the calves throat. When the young heifers were first put out onto fresh pasture they could pick up a lung parasite called Husk, which could lead to pneumonia. The vet had to inject each animal in the lung to kill the parasite, a very painful and uncomfortable procedure, because the professionals claimed it was no good to drench the calf for it would choke.

Ringworms, a form of fungus or wart like skin infection was prominent on the faces of young calves and could be passed onto the workers. Jack would get a bucket or tray of engine sump oil, and with a hand floor scrubbing brush, rub in the oil to prevent the fungus from breathing, causing it to die. One day after stroking the

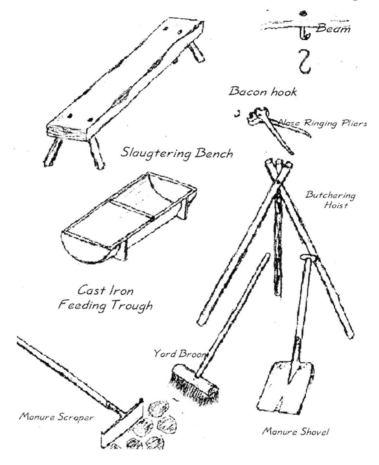

Beam

Bacon hook

Nose Ringing Pliers

Slaugtering Bench

Butchering Hoist

Cast Iron Feeding Trough

Yard Broom

Manure Scraper

Manure Shovel

Plate 2:2 Tools for keeping pigs.

noses of the calves I developed ringworm on my wrist. Using iodine had the same effect.

Giving the animals pills could have proved difficult, but dad made an ingenious devise out of a seven-inch piece of polythene hose or tube, which had a length of bamboo cane snugly fitting down the centre. The inner diameter of the tube allowed the pill to wedge neatly into the end of the tube. Placing the tube in side of the calves' mouth and gently pressing on the end of the bamboo stick dislodges the pill, causing the animal to swallow the pill immediately.

Bags of pig meal were stored in a small wooden fabricated shed inside the engine house next to the bottom barn. Water was collected in a galvanised three-gallon bucket from the one only outside water tap supply. With a home made scoop a portion of grey coloured corn meal was added and rapidly stirred with a well-used well-caked batten of wood. The pigsties were well made with brick walls, and a tiled roof. Inside you would find a row of four inch diameter wooden bars fixed to the walls, positioned six inches away from the floor and three inches away from the wall, as an escape for the piglets so if the sow lay down against the wall, the piglets would not get crushed. In one corner there would be a warm bed of straw under a heat lamp neatly chopped up by the sow to make a comfortable bed. In spite of what people say about pigs wallowing in muck, pigs are clean animals and have good habits. They place all their dropping neatly on the floor on the outer courtyard of the pigsty in the same place, making the daily chore of cleaning easy. The doors have to be hinged and latched to prevent the pigs lifting the doors off their hinges, with their nose. The pigsties were built side by side. The doors to the courtyard were fixed alongside the outer fence, with the feeding troughs built underneath. The feeding troughs were of concrete construction; positioned with a third showing outside the fence, making space to pour the liquid feed from the outside. One needed to keep a vigilant eye on the sow when she was farrowing (when the piglets were being born). If there were a runt or nisgol (small weak piglet) in the litter, it would be put in a fruit box, bedded with a coat on a litter of straw in the wooden annexe next to the store of pig meal under an infrared lamp. Using a bottle fitted with a rubber teat, it would be feed with cow's milk regularly through the day. When it was strong enough it would rejoin the litter.

Soon after the sow had farrowed, Dad would invite me to come and see the freshly born piglets. So as not to alarm the sow he would wait until dusk before he would take me. Standing in the shadows, we would peer quietly over the door. Looking into the dimly lit pen with only a strong infer-red lamp to give added warmth shining in one corner, the sow was laying on her side, with the piglets busily feeding. It was a very peaceful scene except for the occasional grunt from the mother, reassuring her new offspring and the gentle disgruntled squeals from a piglet that had been rousted from a teat.

One or perhaps two nine-month-old pigs would be slaughtered each season for bacon for the farmhouse. Depending on the size of the pig, two to three helpers were needed to lift and hold the pig on the pig bench. Then the local butcher, Arthur Stevenson would knock the pig unconscious using a stun gun and then bleed the pig from the neck. The dead pig would be laid on a bed of straw in the centre of the stable yard. The straw was set alight and the sow rolled over from side to side to burn off the bristles. The pig was then winched up on a three-legged tripod, and carved up into portions. By rubbing a generous portion of salt into the large hams, drawing the moisture out it was well cured. Once all the moisture had been drawn out the final portion of salt was added to preserve the meat over the winter months. Some parts were boiled as ham and others for bacon, with the head and feet (trotters) used for broth.

During the year 1949 the landlord had two bungalows built near to the farm entrance for the farm workers to live in. Willy Price one of the farm workers who lived in one of the farm bungalows decided to keep a few pigs at the bottom of the garden in a purpose built wooden sty. When the day came to take them to Bromyard Market, he managed to load the pigs onto the back seat of his Austin Seven Car, much to everyone's amusement. Winding his way along the main road through the open land of Bringsty Common, the pigs broke through the rear side window, and escaped onto the common. I guess recapturing them was quite an event.

From when Dad took up residence on the farm in 1942 right up to the early 1960's the farm was what we would term a 'general mixed farm' with chickens, ducks, pigs, with grazing land for sheep, beef cattle and suckling cows. The rest of the land was used for growing roots, cereals, corn and fruit orchards.

When Dad and Mum first arrived at the farm, they were welcomed by a flock of white poultry littering the yards and feeding in every area of the farmyard, making an unholy mess in the feeding mangers. The previous tenant Mr. Pugh admitted the hens had been on the farm before he had taken the tenancy, but he would be back to collect them, in the near future.

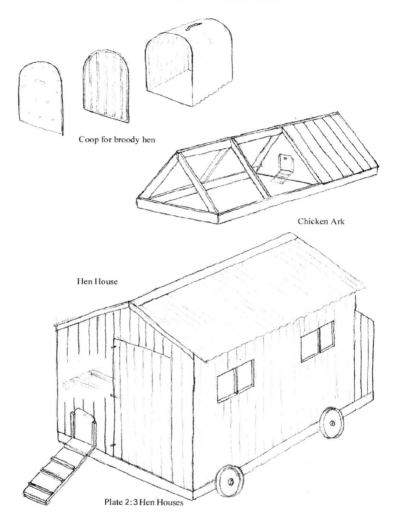

Coop for broody hen

Chicken Ark

Hen House

Plate 2:3 Hen Houses

For Dad, the hens were proving a menace so he decided to set about caging them and then ask Mr. Pugh to collect them. They did not have a poultry house to roost in at night time, so they would fly up into the trees to roost next to the duck pond, which lay at the top of the farm drive. He thought that if he took a light in the dark, he could shine the light onto them in the trees catch them and pen them. But they were very cute, for as soon as he tried to reach them, they just dropped into the pool and to his amazement swam to the edge. So he gave up for a little while.

Dad like all farmers wished to have a sheep dog. One day while in conversation with a visiting cattle and sheep dealer, who he had known from his young days working on the farm at Callow End, asked him while on his travels around the country to look out for a dog a farmer wanting to sell. Some weeks later the dealer arrived with a fully-grown sheep dog from a farmer from the Welsh hills. The sheep dog settled down well, but for a time he did not realise that the dog was deaf.

Because there was no water laid on in the top cattle yard, it was necessary each morning to open the yard gate and drive the cattle up to the top duck pond to drink, and wait while they quenched their thirst. Immediately they had finished drinking Dad would drive them back into the yard. After some days of this routine, one morning having left the cattle to drink Dad went in the farmhouse for breakfast to usefully use his time. Some minutes later he saw the cattle being herded down the drive back into the yard. The dog had watched the cattle drink having seen Dad carrying out the same routine each day, and as soon as the cows had finished drinking, of his own accord driven the cattle back into the yard again.

With the constant intrusion of mangers being messed in Dad decided he would have another go at catching the troublesome hens, with the idea of taking the dog with him to assist, perhaps to corner the hens helping him to catch them easier. With the dog working in the same style as when droving sheep he very soon got the idea of what dad was trying to do. After starting to drive the hens into a corner, to his amazement the dog of his own making would run and lunge at one of the hens, putting his paws on the hens back, then wait for dad to pick it up and put it in the small pen. The job was soon accomplished. The previous tenant was soon round to collect them, knowing Dad had saved him some trouble, and aware of the difficulty needed to catch them.

Each spring Dad would take me out in one of his first cars, either the Ford 8 or later the Austin 12 to the railway station at Knightwick to collect a delivery of day old chickens. At five years of age enthralled by all the excitement I would follow Dad closely into the kitchen wearing my thick grey knee length trousers with braces hidden by a colourful hand knitted jumper, grey hand knitted socks which came up to the knees and a pair of black stiff leathers boots. The chirp of the chicks was enjoyable to listen to as we made our way back through the lanes back to the farmhouse. Once home I would follow him into the kitchen where he would open the lid of the box on the dining room table, and watch the young chicks pecking the saw dust, and grains of food that Dad would have given to them. It was obvious to see the pecking order at just one day old, as certain ones would order the weaker ones around. After a few days when their feathers began to show they would be put in an ark (a portable chicken run). The ark was placed in front of the farmhouse in short grass, where they would get fresh nutrient and rapidly start to grow from a cuddly silky yellow down chick to a maturing young pullet, as the darker coarser feathers began to show through. The chickens were primarily the responsibility of Mum to feed and collect the eggs. Once the chickens started to lay, the older hens would be culled off, making a tasty Sunday dinner. Occasionally one hen would refuse to leave the nest, giving out a repetitive 'clucking' sound indicating that she was 'broody'. She was expecting the infertile eggs to hatch and not wanting to leave the nest, thus giving the show away. You would dutifully pick her up out of the nest, and place her in a single hencoop for a day or two, till the clucking stopped, which indicated she was no longer broody and then you could return her to the hen run again.

During my early years I would spend many happy hours, sitting on an upended large block of fire wood or on the door step of the farmhouse with a hammer in my hand, a stone or brick lay between my legs, as I smashed up damaged crockery into fine pieces, taken from Gran Davies' old panty. As well as corn the chickens were fed with small pellets, and some grit bought commercially in bags, but these chips of crockery were fed to the chickens to help their digestive system. The grit helped grind up the grains of wheat and is used to make the eggshells.

Some years later when I was in my early teens, I had the responsibility of shutting up the hens each night. One morning I went to open up the hen house to be met by hens heads scattered on the ground. Walking a little distance away from the hen house I encountered the bodies of the dead hens, then it suddenly occurred to me. I had forgotten to shut up the hen house door the previous night. The fox had made his nightly visit, found the door open, and had prepared his next month's dinner, by killing them all. When confession time came at breakfast, Mum seemed to keep her thoughts to herself, but Dad did not seem too concerned, as I believe it was a convenient way of closing the chapter on keeping chickens, because no more chickens were kept.

I do recall us having a brood of ducklings by the back door of the farmhouse, but not for long. The ducklings fascinated me so much I would spend time playing with them continually lifting them out of the bowl of water trying to prevent them from stepping in and out and soiling the water. I had not come to realise that ducks lived on water and thrived on it being muddy. Some years later I found out why we did not keep ducks for long, because mum remarked that I had actually drowned some of the ducklings, which I flatly denied. I later discovered that young duckling chicks without a guardian to keep them warm, are not able to get under their mothers feathers to get warm and dry off, so they will die from chill if their downy coats are allowed to get wet. That's my excuse any way, and I am sticking to it.

Chapter 3

Growing root crops.

Tractors. Ploughing and cultivation. Growing and harvesting mangolds, sugar beet and potatoes.

We grew Sugar beet to sell for processing as well as mangolds and swedes used for winter-feed, but it was very labour intensive. In the early days, prior to mechanisation, the farmyard manure was forked onto a horse drawn cart, wheeled up to the field and tipped into piles, to be spread out by hand fork later. It would be ploughed in by horse drawn plough, covering about one acre a day. We had a father and son team working for us with the same Christian names, *Tom* Taylor. Father Tom was known as Mister and his son we called Tom, with both bringing some amusement and excitement on certain occasions. Young Tom seemed to have two left feet when leading the horses, for the horse seemed to be always treading on his foot. At the moment the horse stood on his foot, Tom would shout, *"Wow!"*, to which the horse would dutifully respond immediately, pressing his hoof firmly on young Tom's foot. Tom never did get out of the habit.

The age of the carthorse was drawing to a close, when dad first started farming at Old Gaines farm, yet he was very forward looking and as soon as he could afford it he bought his first tractor, a Standard Fordson. Soon after he replaced it with the Fordson Major, which he purchased with additional tooling that could be lifted hydraulically, using the three points rear linkage. The tooling comprised of a tool bar that fitted on the rear hydraulic three-point linkage where various cultivators and planters could be fitted. Like the earlier Standard Fordson the Fordson Major tractor was started with petrol, and then when it was warm, by switching a two-way tap on the carburettor you would covert it to TVO (tractor vaporising oil) a fuel that is very similar in combustion to paraffin and heating oil. Soon after we purchased the Field Marshal Series 2, one of the first single cylinder diesel tractors.

The Standard Fordson was very difficult to start at times, had no water pump, which gave rise to the water boiling in summer, and did not have a synchronised gearbox. But once you had managed to get it started and once you had crashed it into gear, it proved to be a very reliable tractor. You could use either rubber pneumatic tyres for road use, or steel spade lugs, which gave excellent traction on the soil.

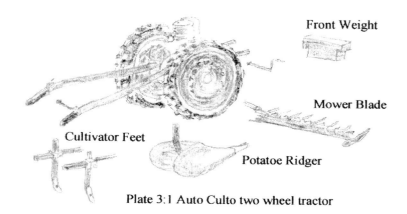

Front Weight

Mower Blade

Cultivator Feet

Potatoe Ridger

Plate 3:1 Auto Culto two wheel tractor

The Fordson Major was also very reliable, but if you had to stop and allow the engine to run idle for any length of time, the moment you pulled out the accelerator lever the engine would stop. Try as you may on the starting handle, but she would not start. All the plugs had built up a layer of carbon, from the unspent fuel. You had to take all four sparking plugs out of the engine, with a spark plug spanner. Then with a wire brush you had to thoroughly clean the plugs, to clear off the build-up of carbon and place a penknife into the spark gap where the spark jumped over in case the bridge was caked up. You then needed to drain the carburettor of TVO fuel, changing back to petrol. She would then happily fire up again. Unwittingly I had the engine cut out on me many times, so whenever I stopped I had to remember to keep the engine running fast if the tractor was to be left running for any length of time.

When I reached 13 years of age, Dad felt confident enough to let me drive the Fordson major unaided. Each spring before the fields were closed up for mowing the rough tufts of grass needed scratching up and the molehills levelled out, using the chain harrows drawn behind the tractor. Chain harrowing was a very

23

simple task needing little skill by crossing to and fro across the field alongside where you had previously driven, so I thought. My first job was to chain harrow the park meadow, opposite the farmhouse. Once I got my confidence in pressing the clutch on the left side of the foot plate and got familiar with the pair of independent brakes on the right side I found that when turning at each end of the field, by applying my foot hard on one of the independent brakes, I could turn in a shorter cycle. Unbeknown to me, glancing over my right shoulder on one of the turns, I saw the harrows being carried up over the rear wheel. Unwisely my first reaction caused me to put out my right hand to unsuccessfully stop the harrows and push them back on the floor. My hand got caught in the links of the chain harrow and started to scrape the skin off the top of my fingers. With panic setting in and my heart beating rapidly, I immediately slammed my foot on the clutch and brakes, without further damage to the harrows or myself. I took little time in discovering that if I used a further length of chain of the right length for towing the chain harrows, I could still take sharp turns without the wheels catching the tyres.

In contrast the Field Marshall was a well-liked and well-respected powerful tractor with excellent traction. This was due to good weight ratio on the rear tyres, filled with water, with soda added to prevent the water from freezing in the winter. The main drawbacks of the tractor was the noisy *thump..thump..pop..pop* from the horizontal single cylinder engine, and the arduous starting options. Diesel engines have no spark plug to ignite the fuel but are ignited by the high compression, so the Field Marshal needed a spark for her to first fire up. At the lower front end of the cylinder head was a threaded hole, to which you inserted a tee bar with a threaded tube, which screwed down into the cylinder head. The starting kit included a 6" long by 2" deep tin containing 2-inch squares of ignition paper. One piece of ignition paper was folded over twice, pushed down into the end of the threaded tee bar. The ignition paper was lit with a match and placed in the threaded tube, screwed back into the cylinder head and the top tee end tapped tight with a hammer. If your driver were a smoker, a cigarette would fit neatly into the threaded tube instead.

On the end of the crankshaft on the right hand side of the engine, was a two-foot diameter by 5 inches wide flywheel made out of solid steel, with a starting handle facility in the centre. On the outer diameter of the flywheel near to the engine was a spiral-threaded groove. Just above the flywheel was a lever with a small guide wheel, which when lifted opened a valve to be able to turn the engine over. Immediately the ignition paper had been inserted in the cylinder head the valve lever wheel was lifted and positioned three threads in onto the flywheel, and the accelerator lever opened by seven notches. Lifting the weighty one and a half-inch diameter solid steel starting handle from its rack on the wheel wing opposite the drivers seat, you would position it into the flywheel. Two men would stand either side of the handle, and on the word, "Go" swing the flywheel three times, immediately drawing the starting handle out of the flywheel, causing the valve lever wheel to fall off the flywheel, allowing the valve in the cylinder head to shut. There was an immediate thump from the engine, with a cloud of black smoke flying out of the tall exhaust as the engine sprang into life. The powerful surge of the horizontal piston *thump..thump.. thump..thump* caused the front the tractor to bounce up and down as if bouncing on a trampoline.

If no one was available to help you start the engine, there was another method. You would go through the same procedure as starting by hand, except you would only put the valve lever wheel on the first thread of the flywheel. On the front top left hand side of the engine, was a tube leading down to the cylinder head. At the top end the tube was threaded and attached was a cast screw cap with a spring-loaded pin in the end. A lever was cast into the cap that you could hit with a hammer to seal the cap tight. Inside the cap you would insert a 12 bore gun cartridge filled only with gunpowder, and the tightened cap. With a sharp tap with the hammer, t hen with one brisk tap with the hammer onto the sprung pin sticking out of the end, the cartridge would give a load bang, which would shoot the exploded gunpowder down the tube into the cylinder head causing the piston to surge back, producing one swing of the flywheel, causing the valve to shut, with the engine springing into life.

At a local farm sale a second hand Field Marshall was included in the auction. Many of the farmers in the area had discovered the qualities of the Field Marshall and were eager to own one. When the Field Marshall came up for bidding a farmer standing close to Dad began passing comments on his Field Marshall he had recently purchased. *"You know,"* said the farmer, *"She's a strange beast to get started in the morning, for when I had horses, I had to feed them first, but with the Field Marshal I have to shoot her first."*

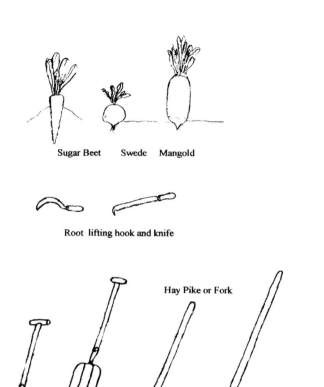

Sugar Beet   Swede Mangold

Root lifting hook and knife

Hay Pike or Fork

Manure Fork

Hay or Sheaf Fork

Potatoe Fork

Fork for Sugar beet and Magolds have less tines

Plate 3:2 Hand Tools for Harvest

The Field Marshal has a large tall exhaust, and during the winter months, when she was doing light work the exhaust would cake up with oily tarry soot. So in spring prior to fieldwork, you would unbolt the exhaust at the base where it fitted onto the engine and lay it on the ground with the top end propped up a few inches off the ground on a log of wood. You would place a wad of loose newspaper up into the lower end soaked in paraffin or petrol, and taking a match set the paper alight. Soon the heat would condense the oily tar and would ignite, in time burning out the oily tarry soot. Once cool the clean exhaust was refitted to the tractor.

The front of the tractor was so balanced to put most of the weight of the tractor onto the rear wheels, so when towing heavy cultivators like disc harrows or a Cambridge Roller up some of the steep slopes over the freshly ploughed, the front end of the tractor would lift slightly with the front wheels only just touching the furrow tops loosing all power to the steering. On the Fordson Major there were a pair of brake pedals side by side allowing you to brake each wheel independently, but with the Field Marshal, alongside each rear mudguard was a tall hand brake lever, in addition to the main hand brake for stopping the tractor and parking. So on steep slopes you would have to let go of the steering wheel and steer with the two independent brake levers, until you were back on level ground.

If Dad had not taken time to spring clean the exhaust on its first hard days work of the season, the driver would look as if he'd had a bad attack of measles, for his face, shirt collar and jacket would be covered in a multitude of oily smuts or spots. On rare occasions at the start of the spring season after an exhilarating hour or two of work the heat of the engine would cause the exhaust to ignite, so you would have to park up and let the engine run idle and wait till the fire burnt out. Leaving the engine running permitted the blast up the exhaust pipe to hasten the fire, leaving the exhaust glowing red-hot. From the age of thirteen I spent up to sixteen hours a day driving the Field Marshal engaged in fieldwork, preparing the soil for planting.

The preparation for planting commenced with ploughing. My early memory of ploughing was of trailing a three furrow Ransom trailer plough with a double spring-loaded safety-towing hitch towed behind the Field Marshal. Bolted to the Field Marshal was an adjustable tow bar that could be moved from side to side connected to an extended shaft up to a steering wheel behind the drivers seat. On the adjustable tow bar was a 'D' link that the plough's safety-towing hitch hooked into. So if the plough hit a large object like a stone the hook on the plough would spring out.

You would always try to turn the plough left-handed when you arrived at the headland. If you were ploughing out a tight corner of the field you may have had no option but to turn the plough around right-handed. It was a hazardous game turning the plough right, because the extra weight of the plough boards or blades would veer to the right and cause an imbalance making it easy for the plough to tip over onto its side.

Before you started to plough up the field you needed a straight parallel line to follow. On most occasions you could begin turning the first furrows in the shallow ridge left from the last seasons ploughing, now showing up as a shallow dip for the right tractor wheel to run in. The right-hand wheel of the tractor was driven in the centre of the shallow ridge with the first of the three mould boards running a shallow furrow of two inches deep behind with the second and third furrow running at full depth.

If you had no ridge to give you a straight start, you needed to take a walk into the nearby coppice and select three straight hazel sticks six feet in length similar to what you would use for growing runner beans. Taking a penknife out of your pocket and making a slit in one end, insert a piece of paper to highlight your marker stick. The three markers were positioned across the field in a start line, in line with one hedgerow, one at each end, and one in the middle of the field. You needed the central marker as a guide to help you as you travelled across the full length of the field, especially if the other end of the field was initially out of sight. Driving along the headland with the plough in tow you turned and positioned the centre of the tractor's front bonnet close to the first stick in line with the second stick. Having removed the first stick you drove the tractor towards the second stick turning a single furrow of three inches deep with the rear mould board. On return the tractor straddled the first furrow, with the second mould board coulter wheel running along the back wall of the previous furrow to create a double width trench, and the rear plough board taking a small slice of soil out from the bottom of the furrow from the previous pass. On the next pass the tractor would then travel back down with its wheel running in the furrow. The first of the three plough boards was unchanged and set to turn a shallow furrow of two inches deep with the second furrow running at full depth to cover the first. On the return, with the front tractor wheel running against the edge of the previous furrow the first of the three plough boards turns a shallow furrow neatly against the face of the previous furrow to produce a neat level set of furrows. On the next pass you would set all the plough boards to their full working depth and commence ploughing in earnest.

As the width of the area that has been ploughed gets wider, and to prevent travelling too far across the headland after each pass you would commence a second fresh opening out some distance across the field, and again continue round and round until you got close to the original area ploughed. Using a well-practiced step you would step out and measure the distance between the two lots of ploughing to ensure that on the last but one pass there was only the width of two furrows left to plough up. It may mean running a narrow furrow behind the tractor wheel on a few passes to get the exact width. Then taking the final pass you would adjust the plough to allow the rear mould board to take just a thin skim of soil out of the third furrow made from the previous pass.

Seeds for growing root crops needed to be planted in good fine loam. Once the ground is ploughed you then drove across the furrows with the Cambridge roll in tow to crack down the furrows, followed by the disc cultivator. In rotation crossing the field in the opposite direction the disc cultivator were followed again by the roller, until you had a good enough loam, taking some days to complete. Soon after the purchase of the Fordson Major Dad bought a rear mounted, power driven rotivator, which fitted directly onto the rear axle of the tractor, driven by the PTO (power take off), lifted by the side arms of the three-point linkage To get the best results the rotivator travelled at a slower pace producing a much finer loam. It produced better results in less time with not having to go over the ground so many times. For roots, especially sugar beet you needed a good depth of soil, so the soil was ridged up, as for potatoes then firmed up with the Cambridge roll in preparation for the seed drill.

The Fordson Major was used to plant the seed, with a set of four seed drills attached to the Tool Bar. The Tool Bar was made up of two angular iron cross bars set 18 inches apart sat along the rear of the tractor, mounted onto the three point linkage. Both lengths of angle had holes every two inches where you could fit various types of tooling. The tool bar had two rubber wheels, which gave you height adjusted. At the rear was a seat and steering wheel, for the operator to steer the tool bar. The steering wheel linkage was attached to the tractor frame. The tooling attachments included seed drills, hoes, cultivators, sugar beet lifters and potato ridging bodies. The set of seed drills, each had an eight-inch square hopper for the seed. Below was a two-foot diameter drive wheel to control the flow of seed, behind which was a vee pointed steel coulter preparing a groove in the ground for the seed to fall into. Behind to cover the seed was another vee shaped steel coulter with a smaller wheel following to firm the soil.

Plate 3:3 Fordson Major E27N

Once the plant had developed two leaves and was approximately three inches tall, a team of workers would hoe out single plants leaving a space of eight inches between giving ample space to grow. Singling the roots take some days to complete. The root crops would need regular cultivation to cut down on the growth of weeds. Again the tractor toolbar was used, fitted with four pairs of 'L' shaped coulters. The coulters were handed one for each side of the row with the horizontal 'L' shape cutting off the weeds. Some seasons the plants would need hoeing a second time if the weeds between the plants grew excessively. Often the proliferation of seeds was caused through farmyard manure containing seed from the previous straw harvest. If there are any signs of farmyard manure in the ground at the time of ploughing, it indicates that the soil is not hungry and healthy. Before Dad purchased the Fordson Major and had the tool bar to cut down the weeds, he travelled the length of the field on foot behind a two-wheeled 'Autoculto' tractor, fitted with just a pair of hoes. The Autoculto only had one gear, which was quite high. It was hard work to keep up with the Autoculto almost having to run up slopes, because he had to have the accelerator well open to get the power. Yet he beavered away, walking behind on foot one row at a time.

Harvesting of roots commenced in October. The sugar beet needed some mechanical aid to dislodge them from the clay soil before lifting by hand because they were so deep rooted. Onto the tractor toolbar was fitted four pairs of 12 inch diameter steel discs. Each pair of discs ran either side of the plants cutting about five inches into the soil. Behind each pair of discs was a pair of coulters, pitched into the ground in a vee, which lifted the plants, causing the plant to rise a few inches, dislodging their roots. To prevent the roots of the sugar beet being damaged by the coulters, someone sat on the toolbar seat to steer.

The second stage of lifting was one of the hardest and most tedious jobs on the farm. Loading farmyard manure into a cart or trailer was hard work but you could keep warm by the energy used and the heat from the manure fermenting, yet when sugar beet lifting you could get extremely cold because you were exposed to extreme weather conditions.

The lifting of sugar beet would continue from October through to the end of January. For the final lifting before putting on your wellingtons you would add an extra pair of fishermen's thick socks. When my father was young you would have worn hob nailed leather boots, over which you would have worn hard leather protective leggings, cupped round your legs with either a row of press-studs or a set of lace up clips. The legs would still need more protection from particles of icy cold soil, and the cutting cold winds that would paralyse your fingers and toes as well as bring a

31

dewy drip to your nose. This would comprise of a large hessian sack tied round your waist with string together with a thick sports jacket and an overcoat on top. Some more hardy workers would work in their bare hands, yet a pair of motorbike gauntlet gloves was very comfortable. Oilskin over trousers used by trawler men replaced the sacking to keep the legs warm, against the cold winds and kept soil out of your wellingtons.

Working up two rows at a time, taking hold of a plant in each hand by the leaves, you pulled the plant out of the soil, then proceeded to knock their roots together to dislodge the soil, neatly laying them down to one side in a row with the leaves facing away from you. A further two rows would be lifted and placed on top, giving sufficient room for a tractor and trailer to pass between for loading. Once sufficient roots had been lifted to fill a lorry you would proceed with the final stage.

With the sugar beet now laying in a straight row, taking a small sickle or beet knife in your right hand, you took the root of the sugar beet in your left hand, then, with two or three sharp blows of the sickle chopped off their leaves with about half an inch of the root crown attached. You could either throw the roots into a pile, to load later, leaving the tops in their rows or a pair of works side by side load them straight into the trailer from either side. The Sugar Beet tops would be left on the ground over the winter months to be collected as and when for feeding to the cattle.

Due to the length of daylight hours there was not sufficient day light hours to get a lorry load together, so it meant working into the evenings by lantern or Tilley light suspended on a pole. Often the lorry would be loaded in the evening, so that an early start could be made to the factory, to get into the unloading queue earlier. It also enabled the driver to get back to the farm before dark to make unloading the hot fresh sugar beet pulp easier.

Swedes were much simpler to lift as they had shallow root systems and could be lifted with out any mechanical aid. Using the spike on the end of the beet hook to dislodge the swede, you took hold of the root with your left hand to cut the leaves off right against the crown. Then with a flip of the wrist you turned the swede round, nipped the slender root off the other end and threw it into a heap. Swedes are quite hardy and will withstand a sharp frost, so could stay in the field over winter. If time permitted it was much easier to load the swedes straight onto a trailer as you lifted them and carted them to the farmstead for storage. Swedes were fed to the cattle and the sheep yet like brussel sprouts needed a frost in them to bring out the sweetness and flavour.

Because of their size and weight mangolds were more difficult to lift and handle. Again they have a very shallow root, with the fourteen inches high body growing above ground. It needed two hands to pick it up after gently leaning it over to detach it from the soil. Then resting it on your knee and holding it steady with your left hand you then grabbed the leaves with your right hand and screw them off, throwing the mangolds into a pile and dropping the leaves on the ground. If you were to cut the mangolds top off in the same manner as other roots, it would bleed and dry up like a rubbery sponge.

Plate 3:4   John and May Hindle with the family

Sugar beet will withstand any amount of frost whereas swedes will only stand a limited amount. Because mangolds carry so much liquid they are frost sensitive and need protection. As an interim measure, if you had to leave the mangolds in heaps in the field you would cover them with their own leaves. Then as soon as it was convenient you would hand load them with a beet fork, into the trailer, take them to the rick yard creating a clamp (a heap) covering it with old spoilt hay, if available. The root fork was similar to the potato fork except it had fewer tines. To prevent damage to the roots or potatoes each tine has a hard marble size

33

steel ball welded to its tip. In later years when hay making and harvesting became mechanised and bailers were in use the clamp was covered with bales of straw.

Comparing sugar beet and swedes, the soil does not need the loam to be so fine for growing potatoes. In the late 1950's we replaced our first rotivator for an orange Howard Rotivator, which worked the full width of the tractor, and much easier to fit onto the three-point linkage. It greatly reduced the amount of time taken to prepare and worked the soil to a good depth.

Next using the tractor toolbar fitted with three vee shaped ridger bodies, the rows or ridges were carved out for planting. The trailer was loaded with Hessian bags filled with freshly purchased Scotch Seed Potatoes together with a dozen or so galvanised metal buckets. With the knowledge of how far a bucket of seed potatoes would span a row, the sacks of potatoes would be strategically placed along the length of the field. The team of planters would space themselves up the length of the field taking a bucket full of potatoes each from the bags placed on the top of the rows. Holding the bucket on the side of the handle with the left hand, with the bucket pitched forward, sitting it on top of the row for support they then began walking with one foot in front of the other in the centre of the row placing the potatoes about twelve inches apart, about one boot length. When Dad thought Paul and I were strong enough to help, he offered us half a crown for each row we planted. In our youthful enthusiasm we would try to out run some of the other workmen, but our energy could not be sustained and we both soon got tired. We are still waiting to be paid!

The next step is to split the ridges to cover the potatoes over using the toolbar ridgers. We could not use the Fordson Major at this stage, because the wheels would have to ride on top of the ridges, compacting the soil, possibly sliding into the bottom of the ridge and damaging the potatoes. It would be impossible to steer the toolbar straight. The little two-wheeled Autoculto tractor came into play fitted with a single potato ridger body. The wheels would run either side of the ridge just avoiding the potatoes. He would run the Autoculto up every other row levelling the top of the ridge so as the Fordson Major tractor could run comfortably along on the top of the rows using the three ridgers to take the ridges to full depth.

The weeds would compete with the growth of the potato plants, so they would need cultivation as soon as any started to show. A set of chain harrows could be passed over the ridges, once or twice to dislodge the seedlings till the potatoes leaves showed through. Once the potato alm (stalks) showed through, then onto the toolbar would be fitted pointed cultivator feet, three to each row. Two would run close to the plant with the other running in the centre of the row bottom.

I was allowed to help steer the toolbar before I was old enough to drive the tractor. To me this was as good as the real thing, so I was always eager to steer, but it had its hair-raising moments. You would need to diligently keep an eye on the plants to avoid the cultivators veering too close and chopping a plant or two off, much to the disgust of dad. Although you were only travelling at two miles an hour, and with total concentration you were not always sure when the tractor was about to reach the end of the row. Whoever was driving dad or John, they would be closely watching the front wheels, and within inches of the hedge or brook, depending which end of the field you were at would brake hard when the wheels touch the side of the hedge or bank of the brook, instantly pulling the lever to lift the toolbar out of the ground, because it was less effort while the tractor was moving. The seat was positioned at the extreme rear of the toolbar suspended on a pair of very long springy lengths of steel plate. Noticing the hydraulic arms of the tractor lifting the toolbar being drawn up out of the ground, I felt as though I was being flung into the air to a great height due to the springing action of the seats suspension. I would have to dig my feet into the footplate and hang onto the steering wheel to prevent me being catapulted off. While I was trying to compose myself the driver would jerk the tractor in reverse, to further dislodge you forward off the seat. Then with his foot hard on one of the independent foot brakes, with the one rear wheel locked, swing the front of the tractor round, causing the toolbar to swing round like a lasso. So if you were not holding the steering wheel tight the steering wheel would slip through your hands with the toolbar flying sideways out of control, throwing you sideways like a pendulum. Before you had got the steering wheel under control the tractor would be again in reverse, with the driver slamming his foot onto the other brake throwing you into the hedge or over the brook as it aligned itself

35

into the next row. Then without warning you felt the toolbar drop to the ground with a thump, finding yourself immediately faced with the row of plants, instantly having to quickly realign the toolbar and off to go. With a smile on his face the driver would occasionally gave a turning glance to see your panic ridden face, and then try to manoeuvre the tractor a little more sedately.

The cultivator would need to pass through the rows of potatoes a number of times to keep the weeds down. Then the ridger bodies would again be fitted onto the toolbar, to make the final pass of moulding the soil up to the plants, leaving them to mature till harvest time in the Autumn.

Potato harvest commenced in mid-October to coincide with the school half term, when the alms (stems) have died and are lying on the ground wilted white and brittle. Potato lifting had to be done by hand and is backbreaking work, yet the women folk in the surrounding villages were always willing to do some casual work to earn a few extra coppers. The team of workers would turn up on the first day, having heard through word of mouth, then for the duration of the harvest be collected and taken home again in the farm van. Half an hour before they were due to arrive the tractor and trailer was loaded with empty bags and buckets, and if allowed I would sit on the bags and have a ride to the field. The bags would be strategically placed down between the rows with a bucket to each set of bags, to which one picker would be allocated. Once the bags and buckets had been unloaded the tractor would then unhitch off the trailer and then be attached to a converted horses drawn potato lifter.

The tractor driver would commence lifting three rows in for the first few bouts to prevent the machine throwing the first row of potatoes into the hedge. The lifter had a wide blade that sliced right under the row, and attached behind was a wheel driven propeller shaped like a 'spider's web' that rotate and scatter the potatoes out to the side of the row. If you could get enough pickers, you could keep the potatoe lifter circling round and across a dozen rows up and down, so as soon as the pickers had finished their section they would stride across the untouched rows to the other side and work their way back up the other row just lifted.

Before the introduction of the mechanical digger, a pair of horses would tow a single ridger body, with each side coulter formed into fins, shaped like the spread out wings of a bird, allowing the soil to fall through, pushing the potatoes to one side. Not all the potatoes would show up so a lot of scratching in the soil with your bare hand had to be done to hopefully get every potato.

If you were walking along the side lane adjacent to the field you could not mistake the distinct sound of metal buckets being raised and lowered on top of the ground and the metallic sound of potatoes being thrown into the bucket, or being deposited into the Hessian sacks. The distinct chatter and contagious laughter egged on by one of the ladies explaining some anecdote would also add to the rhythm.

One of the helpers Jim Overton lived on Bringsty Common adjacent to the farm, till he had to give up through ill health. Meanwhile his wife Phyllis continued to help both with potato and cider fruit picking. As potato picking coincided with the school half term the mothers used to bring their young children with them. One of Phyllis' children had a tendency to wander so Phyllis would tie the child up with a liberal length of string to a hedgerow or gate. One potato-picking season Phyllis' child could be heard shouting from the lower end of the field out of earshot of his mother. One of the men folk who was lower down the field and nearer the child could hear and understand what the child was saying. Mimicking the child's voice he shouted "*Mummy I want a wee-wee!*". Mum raced down the field and unceremoniously made the child comfortable where she was tied up to the contagious laughter of all.

When finishing time was imminent the tractor would again be hitch up to the trailer. John Hindle who had joined the farm as a young Lancashire man did most of the tractor driving. Together with Jack they would load the bags of potatoes onto the trailer. John was left handed, so together standing either side of the sack, they would draw the top of the bag of potatoes back a little as they faced the trailer. One would take a 2-foot long length of wood taken from the end of a broken hayfork handle and place it across the lower back of the sack. Each would take a firm hold of the top corners of the sack with one hand, leaning it right back with the main weight of the sack leaning onto the pole, then together lifting the sack and swinging it onto the trailer. The loaded trailer could be taken to the entrance to the field and the bags emptied making a long domed heap 6 foot high, called a clamp, which later would be covered with a layer of spoilt dry hay followed by thin layer of turf, to keep the frost out. Alternately the potatoes were taken to the farm implement shed where the sacks would be emptied. This building had a south facing entrance and thick brick side walls greatly reducing the access to frost, yet we still added a layer of hay, and when available used bales of straw instead.

Some potatoes would escape the lifter having still been covered with soil when the lifter passed, so the cultivator used prior to keep the weeds at bay while the plants were young, was used to scuffle the ground to bring the rest to the top, with everyone joining in to collect them. The full time workers did have one little perk at this time. They were allowed one row of free potatoes for themselves, which adequately kept them through the season.

Once the soil on the potatoes had dried out, and no imminent sign of frost, they were sorted and weighed, then were sold to and collected by the local seed merchant J. W. Williams of Bromyard. For many seasons the potatoes were sorted by hand but the availability of a potato-sorting machine, was much quicker and easier. Three operators were required, one to fork the potatoes in, one to stand over the riddle and throw out the damaged ones and one to change over the bags when full. Using a potato fork the first person would load the potatoes onto a pair of electrically driven 2 foot by 4 foot long shaker sieves. The top sieve was of 2-inch square mesh and the lower one of 1-inch square mesh. The second operator would watch for damaged or rotten tubers, throwing the rotten ones into one bucket while the damaged ones would eventually be bagged up for use in the farm kitchen. The top sieve would transport the good potatoes onto a twin pair of conveyors, which would be shut off alternately as the Hessian bags filled. The potatoes off the lower sieve would be collected for feeding to the pigs, while the soil, small stones and anything smaller would fall to the ground, to be shovelled up at the finish. The third operator would be busy changing the bags and weighing them into half hundredweights ready to have the tops sewn up.

For sewing the tops up you would use a slightly curved bagging needle with a length of binder twine, the string used to tie up sheaves of corn. You would lap the top of the sack over a couple of times first, then passing the needle through under the fold about 3 inches in from end slip the string twice round the end piece to form an ear. You would then sew round the fold working toward the opposite end, curving the string to create an ear the other end, finally tying it off.

The pig potatoes as required were tipped into a large boiler of four-hundredweight capacity measuring 3 feet in diameter by 4 feet high. It had a couple of gallons of water put in first up to a mesh platform sitting about 4 inches off the base. The potatoes would be steamed for 3 to 4 hours. To tip the potatoes out easily, the boiler sat on a tubular steel frame, which allowed it to be easily pivoted. When cold the potatoes were fed either on their own to the pigs or mixed with a portion of meal.

Chapter 4

Haymaking and Harvesting

All the root crops were rotated from field to field each year. If a field had been growing roots for some years, it would be seeded down with a well-chosen type of grass and clover for a well-needed rest. As well as having good nutritional value clover produces a bulky heavy crop.

Before planting the grass seed the ground would be ploughed and cultivated in the normal way to a fine loam. Granulated fertilizer, with slag (potash) would be spread using a specially made spreader with a wide wooden hopper. Along the length of the hopper base was a pair of slotted steel plates. The width of overlap in the slots were adjusted to control the flow of fertiliser to the soil. In the early days, the slag was delivered in fine hession sacks, which produced vast amounts of dust, getting itself into everything, but soon changed to paper sacks. In more recent times to prevent the slag getting damp and changing into a solid stone the slag was supplied in one cwt polythene bags.

In bygone days the grass seed was sowed by hand, with the worker strutting across the field spreading the seed out in front in a fan shape. The seed was carried in a purpose built kidney shaped hopper, which sat on his thigh and tucked under his one arm with a strap slung over his shoulder to take the main weight. Later the hopper was replaced with the fiddle, so named because the seed was spread with a fan shaped disk propelled by a leather string bow similar to the type used on a violin. Dad would pick up the fiddle and throw a strap around his neck attached to an eight-inch square hopper, which he slung under the one arm. On the top edge of the hopper was attached the upper part of a small hession sack to extend the hopper and enable you to carry more seed. Attached to the base was a pair of circular steel slotted plates, acting as shutters, smaller but similar to the ones used on the fertilizer spreader. Again a small lever was attached to open and close the slots to control the feed of grass seed. Below the feeder fitting into a hole in the centre was a wooden shaft or spindle, with its other end attached to the base of the fiddle. Near to the base of the hopper where the seed flowed out was a shaft driving a circular plate with fins, which when turned to and fro, would by centrifugal force distribute the seed. Then taking the bow, which comprised of a three-foot length of one inch dowelling, attached a length of leather strap to a knob on one end. The strap was passed once round the wooded shaft holding the metal propeller, before being attached to the other knob. So by taking hold of one knob in the right hand and drawing the bow to and fro the finned disc would distribute the seed.

Plate 4:1 David in the hay field

Dad would then take a couple of hazel sticks, about six feet in length, from the hedgerow, or use the set of sticks used for marking out for ploughing. With his penknife he would make a point on one end and make a four inch split in the other in which he would place a piece of white paper. The sticks would be stuck in the ground; at about four feet intervals along either end the field

41

parallel to the hedgerow, as guides. Then in a controlled three-foot long stride he would stride across the field in a straight line from one marker stick to the other. Once he had arrived he moved the stick forward 4 feet, before aiming back towards the other stick, back at the other end of the field.

Once the seeds had been sown, the final job was to cover the seed with a set of chain harrows, followed by the Cambridge Roll to firm up the soil.

The fields allocated for hay would need to be closed off to livestock towards the end of March, to allow time for the grass to grow. Over the past year since the last time it was mown, molehills will have appeared, and cowpats would have left bald patches and burnt the grass. The set of chain harrows would be towed over the pasture once to level the molehills and break up the cowpats.

The right time to cut grass for haymaking was when the grass was in full ear and still lush green. To make good quality hay, you needed up to four good days of hot sunshine, with a gentle breeze to waft the swathes of grass to aid the drying.

To get an idea of the weather pattern for the next few days, you would wisely listen to the shipping forecast on the Radio, or keep a watch on the cloud formations. The wise proverb, 'Red Sky at night Shepherds delight', invariably promises a good day to follow.

For generations, since iron was discovered, the cutting of grass was carried out by hand with the scythe. The men worked in teams, and as you passed by the field, even if you did not see them, you could hear the regular metallic sound of the sharpening stone being drawn down each side of the blade to and from the handle, to keep the blade razor sharp. Then you would hear the sliding action of the scythe, as the blade glided just above the ground, in a swinging half moon formation, taking about two inch width of grass at each swipe, to create a neat swathe to one side.

In my early childhood years, the farmers were using horse drawn mowers. There was a seat on the mower, where the horseman would sit, to steer the horses. The mower had two cast iron wheels that drove the cutter blade. Soon after the same design of mower had the horse shafts replaced with a tractor drawbar. The five-foot cutter bar, which lay on the right side of the mower comprised of a set of sharp pointed coulters, fitted onto a heavy flat steel base. Passing through the coulter slots was the cutter bar. The cutter bar comprised of a length of rectangular steel onto was riveted a set of triangular cutter blades, pointing forward. With a scissor action against the coulters, the cutter bar would cut the grass by being driven to and fro. A wooden swathe board was attached at the far side of the mower cutter body, slightly pitched towards the mower, to draw the grass away from the uncut grass, to prevent the cut grass entangling with the mower on the next bought to be cut.

The blade would need to be replaced or sharpened at least twice a day, depending on the coarseness of the grass and the weight of the crop. A second blade was carried to the field to save on sharpening time, or replacement if a blade broke or was damaged. With a heavy crop, or if there was a chance of stone damage, the blade would often need replacing more than twice, having to sharpen or repair the blade in the field. As part of the kit you needed to carry a Claw Hammer and a small quantity of four inch round nails. Two nails would be driven part way into the top rail of the wooden gate, about three feet apart. The blade would be placed in front of the two nails, and then the nails were bent over firmly onto the cutter bar. Two further nails were driven in, in front, in the inner cleft of two of the blades to hold the cutter bar firmly. Standing behind the blade the edges of the blades were sharpened with a smooth flat file, drawing the file away from the operator. Once complete it was just a matter of twisting the bent rear nails to one side with the claw hammer, to release the cutter bar.

If it was a thin, light crop, by early afternoon the top layer of the swathe was dry and ready for turning. In my young days, and in the early days of the scythe, I can remember turning the hay by hand, with a two-pronged hayfork. A team of workers would take a row each, walking behind each other, turning the swathe over into the path of the row that had been turned over by the person in front. Although I was only five years of age my first happy memory of turning hay by hand was joining the team as they worked their way around the Park Meadow opposite the farmhouse next to the farm buildings. One haymaking season, after cutting the grass we discovered this same field had an infestation of grass snakes, breeding all over the field. As the grass was cut, the snakes made their escape, moving into the yards and

43

buildings. Some endeavour was made to unsuccessfully destroy them, but after a couple of days they dispersed into the undergrowth around the edge of the farm buildings. Few snakes, of any species have ever been seen since, on any part of the farm.

During Hay making time the days were very long with everyone rising early before sunrise. A team of horses with a mower driven by its steel wheels would leave the farm early and mow till breakfast by which time the sun would have dried up the dew. Then after breakfast the grass cut the previous day was turned over, allowing the underside to dry. If there were a crop of hay completely dry, then it would be prepared for collecting. In the early days of horses it was common to arrive for work for 5.00am to feed the horses, then set out to the field at 6.00am to start mowing. In the first two years at the farm, dad used a horse drawn hay side turner, to turn the hay. The side turner had two large steel spoked drive wheels. In front of each wheel was a large dish shaped disc. The discs were joined by a set of four equally positioned angle iron supports which each had a line of spikes pointing to the ground. The drive wheels drove one of the discs, which in turn rotated the sets of tines. The set of discs and tines were positioned at an angle, so as the turner was drawn along, the rotating tines turned the grass over drawing it to one side. In the early day's the turner was towed by horses but was soon replaced with a tractor drawn type. There was a lever at the front to lift the tines from the row, but because of its rigid construction, when it passed over very uneven or hollow patches of ground it would miss some of the hay, so you had to have an extra helper to follow up behind in places to assist. The grass would need turning up to four times for a heavy crop. If the crop were dense and heavy, a team would still need to go over again by hand to shake the swathe up to expose the damp wads of grass in the centre to reach the suns heat. If the weather was inclement, with unpredictable rainstorms, it could take many more turns to get it dry.

The pride of the farmer is being able to collect the hay, when it is still a beautiful lime green and has a very rich sweet smell. Rain storms, can at one go, turn the stalks black, and in an inclement season, having been turned many times, turn to a pale brown, with all the nutrients burnt out, ending up only good enough for bedding. Its only use is as a stomach filler in very cold winter times, or a covering for the mangold or potato clamps.

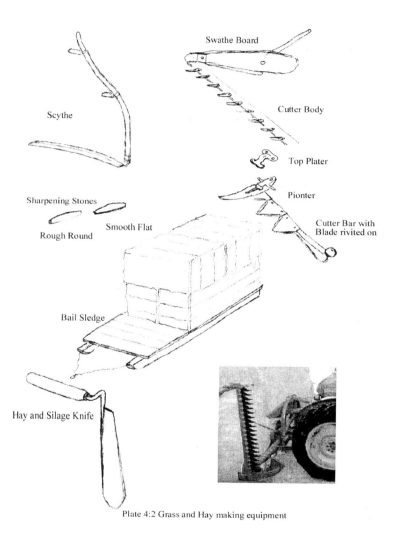

Swathe Board

Scythe

Cutter Body

Top Plater

Sharpening Stones

Pionter

Rough Round   Smooth Flat

Cutter Bar with
Blade rivited on

Bail Sledge

Hay and Silage Knife

Plate 4:2 Grass and Hay making equipment

Paul and I could not wait for the Park meadow to have the hay crop cleared. It left low stubble with no cowpats to tread in, so we would be out there with John and Willy's children from the farm bungalows, to play cricket, or football. When playing cricket, it was always hard to decide whether to use a tennis ball or cricket ball. As I got older I felt more confident to use the cricket ball, not fearing so much of getting hit. The very thought of asking Mum if she could purchase a protective kit, would automatically be answered with, *"Too expensive, you'll soon get tired of wearing them"*. So inevitably we would use a tennis ball, which would do its own thing when it hit the ground, a hole or the stump from a clump of dock leaves. When hit hard the ball had a tendency to travel a great distance, ending up over the fence or hedge. The games were quite often short lived and frustration soon set in, trying to hunt the ball after a considerable amount of time was spent with the bat, rummaging through clumps of nettles, ending up with our unprotected legs well stung.

In the early days the hay was collected using horses. The horse would be tethered to the front of a hay sweep. The sweep which lay on the ground was like a large fork made up of a dozen two inch square poles, spaced about five inches apart, with steel spokes attached to the sharp end. The rear ends of the poles were attached to an upright gate like structure, with two handles for the horse hand to steer the sweep, together with joe lines to guide the horse to the hay swathe. With the steel ends pointing forward the horse towed the sweep up through and along the rows to collect the hay. Once full the sweep was towed back to the rick, which was being built in the field. The horse hand, approaching the rick, lifted the handles of the framework, causing the spikes of the sweep to dig into the ground, with the frame of the sweep rolling over top of the pile of hay. Then due to the way the sweep was balanced, fell back the right way up, ready for the next collection. A year or two later, dad bought a sweep of similar design to the horse drawn model to be pushed in front of the Field Marshal.

Very soon the level of the rick was out of reach for the workman throwing the hay up onto the top so an elevator was towed up against the rick. Sets of wooden paddles coupled by a pair of chains were driven up the platform of the conveyor by a petrol engine positioned underneath. Each paddle had three, seven-inch spikes sticking up which caught the hay or sheaves of corn and drew it up the conveyor. For ease of manoeuvrability and transport, the overreach of the conveyor could be collapsed in half, using a winch mechanism, with a pair of vertical gantry's one either side. The two gantries once upright were used to position the platform at an angle; in it's working position. To transport the conveyor again, once the task was complete the platform was lowered to the horizontal, then the base of platform was unbolted halfway along. Again the gantries would be used to winch the upper half of the platform, by a hinge to lower the top section onto the lower section reducing the length of the conveyor by half. In early times a horse driven Ginny ring drove the conveyor. This comprised of a drive shaft leading from the conveyor up to a gear mechanism centrally mounted with a wooden shaft or yoke attached rotated by a horse, circulating around the gear mechanism.

Some of the hay was brought home, loaded onto a horse drawn dray by hand with two tined hayforks and stacked in a rick opposite the Dutch barn back at the farmstead. The Dutch barn was used only for storing the sheaves of corn.

In an inclement damp season, if you could not get the hay fully dry, it would heat up in the stack through fermentation, and because the main of the rick was dry, would ignite, through the amount of heat generated. To ensure the hay is sufficiently dry and ready for collecting up form the field, you would crack open the joints on the stem, to ensure there is no sign of moisture.

One season when I was still very young I do recall the fire brigade being called out to the hayrick. It had not gone on fire, but there was a very strong smell of burnt hay coming from the Rick. The firemen inserted a steel thermometer, to determine how hot it had got. Fortunately it was not too hot to ignite, so by gently dismantling the rick, the main of the rick was saved.

Soon after Dad came to live at the farm, mechanical stationery balers were invented and were available for hire. We hired our first stationary baler from Jack Smith a contractor from Pencombe, a little village west of Bromyard. The baler was towed into the field behind an orange coloured Case LA tractor driven by his employee George Baynham. The tractor drive pulley, was connected up to the large fly wheel of the baler by a 5" wide belt to drive the baler. The sweep in front of the Field Marshal was drawn up in front of the baler, and then the hay was forked into the high wide hopper by hand. Steel spikes sticking up through slots in the hopper platform, drew the hay towards the centre chamber. At the point of where the hay came to the chamber a nodding horses head that pushed the hay into the heart of the baler. Immediately the horses head came up, a trolley like ram, running on wheels along a tunnel of four angle iron girders, drove the hay tightly into the rectangular bale chamber at intervals, before the ram returned to compress the next wad of hay After the hay had reached about 3' 6" in length a workman standing alongside drove a large 'U' shaped steel fork into the bail tunnel across the face of the bale between the bale and the ram, along a pair of guide channels. A small channel ran along the outside of each spike of the fork where a pair of 10-foot long steel wires were passed through to the other side of the chamber. The wire was then threaded back through the previous fork in front of the previous bale, and then with the wire a little slack, the start of the wire was looped through a loop at the other end and joined to make one complete bale. As the bale was slowly thrust out through the end of the baler chamber by the thrust of the ram trolling back and forth, the bale would expand enough to tighten the slack wire ties. The hand that was responsible for tying the bale wires lifted the bale off the ground, using handspikes and either stacked them in the field near to the baler or loaded them onto a dray, to haul back to the rick yard.

Come mid-morning and mid-afternoon, Mum would take a well-earned cup of tea up to the field. Back at the farmhouse, Mum would fill two or three large glass juice bottles full of tea, collect some cups, and if it was late afternoon, cover in grease proof paper a bundle of tomato, plum or currant jam sandwiches into a tea towel, drop them into a basket, with either Paul or Jane inside the pram, with one hand carrying the basket, and walk up to the field. As it was so hot, the tea would not always be drunk straight away. The cold tea was very refreshing to drink and relished by everyone, being a great thirst quencher.

By the time I was old enough to understand farming methods, changes had started to take place in haymaking. Soon the tractor sweep and the stationary baler were retired. Now once the hay was dry the side turner towed by a tractor would straddle one row of hay, bringing a second row of hay alongside together to make them into one. Jack Smith had now purchased one of the first mobile tractor drawn New Holland pick-up balers. The baler towed behind the Case tractor was a very heavy and an extremely wide machine to transport from farm to farm. Before the baler could enter any of our fields, we had to remove the earth from around the gateposts and lean them to one side, in order to get the baler through. To release George Baynham to other work dad was often asked to drive the Case tractor and bale up the hay himself, and visit other farms in the locality and help bale their hay also.

Plate 4:3A Jack Perrigo & Jim Overton waiting by Hay Baler

At hay making and harvesting I did enjoy walking up the lane with Mum to the field with the refreshments. All the workers would make their way to the field entrance, as Dad pulled up alongside with the noisy loud hum of the tractor and baler engines and the thump, thump of the ram in the bale chamber, shutting down to a very peaceful quiet, and well-earned break. One or two of the workers would draw together a few bales to form a circle

49

and we then sat on them to enjoy a pleasurable picnic. With the warm sun shining on us, and the rich smell of dried hay, it was sheer joy being in the field, in amongst all the buzz of activity. Once work recommenced, I would persuade Mum to let me follow the baler round the field for a while. Occasionally, travelling along a slope, as the bales left the baler they would fall into the next row to be baled, so I would get some joy pushing them back to allow the baler to pass without having to stop.

Plate 4:3B Haymaking using sweep in front of
Field Marshal

Following close behind the baler Jack and John would begin to stack the bales in pairs, four layers high. The first two bales were stacked on their side to allow the air to pass through and minimise the damp rising into the bales. The job of loading the bales onto the dray or trailer was an art, like the loading of loose hay, in the early days. For me, those early days of haymaking were one of the most pleasurable times of the year. Haymaking conjured up warm sunny days, with good social times in the field during the tea breaks, encompassed with the smell of either fresh mown grass, or the aroma of rich lime green drying hay, with the hum of fly's, and the swirling, whistling sound of swallows in the air diving to catch insects for their young. I am saddened that this traditional form of farming in this country may have been lost forever.

By the middle of the 1950's Jack Smith decided to retire and sell up his business, which meant us having to find another contractor. Watkins and Griffith were the obvious choice as they were based only four miles away, in Bromyard, and as Stan Griffith was living in our village, he was close at hand to travel to us.

It was unpredictable as to when and if the contractor would turn at the time when the crop was ready for baling or harvesting. Quite often other farmers had contacted them before you, so you were now in the queue, and by the time they arrived the crop could have been rained on, or past it's best.

Although finances were very tight at this time, Dad managed to persuade the bank to give him a loan, to buy some haymaking machinery. His intensions were to do some contracting with the new machinery in order to help pay off the bank loan, as well as guaranteeing getting his own hay making done, in fine weather and in good condition. So in exchange for the Fordson Major, and the Field Marshal he bought a Fordson Super Major, a three-point linkage grass mower and a New Holland 67 hay Baler.

For one or two seasons he borrowed a bale sledge to be drawn behind the baler. A worker would stand on the front half of the sledge if the field was not too steep, stacking the bales on the rear end of the sledge two bales wide by four high. Then by a gentle push the rear of the sledge would tip, and the stack of bales would gently slip onto the ground behind. We then purchased a mechanically operated sledge, which was made up of an open frame with a set of two-inch wide belts attached to the front frame spaced at about six inches apart, which trailed along behind on the ground the full width of the sledge. The bales would fall into the centre of the framework sliding along on the ground, along the top of the belts, finishing up against the gate at the rear. When the driver saw that the sledge was full, he would pull a cord, which would unlock the gate, which hinged into the air, allowing all the bales to passed through underneath re-shutting itself by its own weight. The bales would still have to be stacked afterwards, but at least they were all together, making it easier to load them onto the trailer.

We gained quite a lot of haymaking business around the area, which helped much with the finances. By now I could confidently drive the tractor, although I would have to wait till I was sixteen, before getting a provisional licence, to drive on the road. During school holidays Dad would drive the machinery to the neighbouring farms, and I would ride behind on my bicycle. Once I had got started Dad would ask the farmer to give him a lift back home, to get on with milking and attending to the dairy herd.

As soon as I was sixteen, I applied for a licence to drive the tractor. Once I had the licence, I could not drive the tractor on the road until I had a test. So I immediately, applied for the test. On the day of the test, the examiner drove to a local location, and arranged to meet me with driving the tractor using 'L' plates. He then just asked me to carry out the more elementary manoeuvres, using the correct hand signals, and then handed me the document, which you automatically assumed said you, had passed, but only to drive a tractor on the public highway. I had to apply for another provisional licence when I was seventeen to drive a car. But this provisional licence covered both farm tractors and cars.

We now met with a slight draw back when it came to the final stage of baling the hay. We had sold all the old tractors yet we needed a tractor to continue to row in the two rows of hay in front of the baler. This meant either borrowing a tractor or have to keep swapping the Super Major over from one machine to the other loosing valuable time and effort.

One of the farmers in the village had sold a Fordson Major Model KFD to an agent in Worcester, J. C. Baker. This particular model was for orchards with low-slung trees, and had smaller wheels than the standard Fordson Major diesel, with the exhaust pipe slung underneath. For a modest price we bought the model KFD, which came to be known as 'Dolly' giving us many years of faithful service. He later purchased a Vicon Leyley side turner hay rake, which was made up of four sprung tined wheels, running in a line at 45 Deg to one another, to row up the hay. This machine was able to work at a very fast rate over the ground, and as it was three point linkage mounted had good manoeuvrability, to keep ahead of the baler.

After leaving school at 15 I worked on the farm for just 18 months. I then took a career in Engineering, so my brother Paul took my place.

Plate 4:4 Break time

In an inclement season the hay can get spoilt and be very unpalatable, so as an alternative farmers started to silage the grass. The grass would be cut needing a little time to wither, and then could be collected straight away, as long as no rain had fallen on it. In the mid 1960's the summers were very wet, so we purchased a green crop loader, which travelled behind the moving trailer straddling the path of the mown grass. The green crop loader comprised of a wooden platform set at 45 deg, which allowed the grass to be conveyed up and onto the trailer. A set of wooden paddles, with spikes attached, driven by the ground wheels, dragged the grass up, dropping the grass onto the bed of the trailer. The trailer that had one thripple or extension on the front had a worker riding on top, who stacked the grass in place with the same art and skill needed to load sheaves of corn. Back at the farm, a clamp or pit was dug out about four feet deep, using the soil for walls, where the load was dispatched. A tractor at the clamp, with the aid of a large fork, mounted to the three-point linkage would carry the grass up into a neat pile. The tractor would then make a number of runs over the grass to press it down to remove all air. By becoming airtight, and with a vinegar spray added, the grass would pickle instead of rotting down. Once full the clamp was covered with plastic sheet, and held down with tyres.

In winter when the silage was needed for feeding, a hay knife was used to cut the silage, and then it was transported to the cattle or sheep on the back of the tractor by a three-point linkage lift box or trailer, to be spread on the field, or fed to them in the cattle fold manger.

Corn could be planted either early autumn or spring depending on the variety of corn we bought. Of the three types of corn we chose to grow wheat and oats, but my uncle Geoffrey back in Hoarwithy grew mainly barley. By planting autumn corn it meant we would be able to harvest a week or two earlier. Harvesting in the early days was very labour intensive and lengthy, so by spreading out the planting time, it would give more time to get the harvest in. We grew wheat to sell, with the residue of small corn seeds used to feed the hens. The oats were either stored in hession Godsell Brown sacks, which could hold 2.1/4 cwt, or loose on the granary floor, and then ground up for winter animal feed.

For growing corn the ploughed soil needed to be cultivated to a medium tilth, with granulated fertiliser added. Every four to five years the soil would need feeding with lime, to add calcium and to keep the soil healthy. As still happens today, contractors still travel from farm to farm with tractor and lime spreader, followed close behind by a lorry that will discharge the lime into the spreader. In the early 1950's the granulated fertiliser, was spread using its own spreader, but in later years the corn drill had a twin hopper, which could house the corn and fertiliser side by side. The flow of corn was regulated by a drive from the wheels and fell into a metal tube, which was made out of coiled steel plate allowing it to spring up and down with the profile of the ground. Running shallow in the ground below each spout, set at a slight angle, was a dished disc, which drew the soil to one side to allow the corn and

54

fertiliser into the row or drill behind. It was necessary for a second operator to ride on the back of the early single hopper seed drills or corn planters, to disconnect and reconnect the planters drive mechanism at each and of the field. On the rear was a 6" wide duckboard, similar to a builders plank, running along the rear of the drill about 9" off the ground, but for some unknown reason, it was set on a slight tilt tipping backwards. Positioned along the rear of the hopper was a long lever. When you reached each end of the field, you swung the lever over from one side of the planter to the other, which lifted the seed drills out of the ground, and disengage the drive. You needed to ride on the duck board to work this lever, and because of the precarious tilt on the duck board you had to travel with your hand firmly anchored to the lid handle, to stop falling off, which was very tedious and hazardous. I was often asked to ride on the seed planter, so because I was young at the time and not very strong, so the tractor had to invariably stop each time to enable me to disengage and engage the lever. When the planter was full of corn the lever was hard to move, with me having to step down off the planter to draw the lever over and down to its full position. As soon as the lever was in its correct position the tractor operator would be off again, with me hastily run behind to jump back onto the precariously fitted running board and hang on to the lid to stop myself falling off. After the field was planted, a set of Spike Harrows would be towed over the ground by a tractor to cover the seed followed by the Cambridge Roll to firm the soil down. Apart from building a scare crow out of disguarded clothes, and the occasional gun shots from a twelve bore gun to stop the crows and pigeons eating the grain during the early days of germination, no more work was needed till harvest. In later years when the corn was half grown, sprays were used to keep down the weeds.

When harvesting was imminent, Dad and I would walk up the lane and stalk between the rows amongst the ripened field of corn. He would choose one or two strategic places in the field particularly areas which were sheltered, where the corn had been slower to ripen. He would pluck an ear of corn and place it into his cupped hands, and roll the ear between the two palms to dislodge the grain, blow away the chaff, and then pop the seeds into his mouth. If the corn was of a soft milking texture, it was far from ripe, but if a precarious amount of pressure was needed between the teeth to break the grain, resulting in a firm crack when it broke, it meant that it was stone dry and free from moisture, indicated it was ready for harvest. In later years as farming became more sophisticated, the ripeness of the corn was determined by placing a few grains in a tube, and passing an electric current through it. The rate of conductivity with which the electric passed through the grain would determine the moisture content, and as to how dry the grain was.

Plate 4:5 Case LA Tractor and New Holland Baler

My earliest recollections of harvesting was when I was around the age of four, accompanying John up to the Snygmore field of ripe wheat, taking with him a corn hook and sickle. He needed to cut a wide enough strip around the edge of the field to allow the tractor and binder to make its first pass around the field. Wending his way round the edge of the field, he drew the standing corn stalks to one side with the wooden hook in his right hand swiping at the base of the stalks with the sickle in his left hand, until he had enough stalks cut to make a sheaf. Taking a separate handful of stalks he wrapped them round the sheaf, tucking and folding the ends into one another to bind the sheaf tight. He then would lean the sheaf against the hedge or fence, and begin to cut the next sheaf. I had not as yet started school, but was very inquisitive watching all that was happening on the farm, and constantly learning. I vividly remember John saying that the stalks were brittle, so I asked him to explain the meaning, to be told the stalks broke easily.

In the early years at the farm, Dad hired a corn binder, towed by horses, but soon bought a horse drawn model for himself. After a year or two he then purchased a tractor drawn 'Albion' model, which gave him good service for some years, which he towed behind the Fordson Major E27N. The corn binder has a cutter bar similar to the grass mower. High above the blade is a set of rotating flails, which draw the corn heads over onto a 4 feet wide moving horizontal canvas conveyor. A second canvas conveyor rising at 45 degs takes the corn up and over into a collecting point at the side of the machine. When the bundle is large enough, a piece of string attached to a curved needle passes around the sheaf, and the string is knotted, immediately being slung to one side by a pair of tines, onto the ground. After the binder has travelled round three to four times round the field, there was room for a team of workers to stack the sheaves against on another in pairs into sets of six or eight sheaves called a stook. The sheaves would be at a slight angle touching at the top so that a tunnel was formed to let the air through to dry out the stalks, or any grass or weeds that was mingled with them. If there was no green foliage intermingling with the stalks, wheat and barley could be hauled to the rick more or less straight away, but the grain oats were always ripe before the stalks and stayed out for up to three weeks, before hauling to the barn or rick, to avoid the rick heating up and going on fire. Some seasons you would constantly have to stop and draw stinging splinters out of your hands, if you were carrying sheaves into stooks, which had a high proportion of thistles in them. As you picked up the sheaf by the hand, tucking them under each arm, for ease of carrying them to the stook, the underneath of your wrists and arms where it is most tender, would get scratched from the ears of corn and the sharp ends of the stalks.

In an inclement season while waiting for the corn to dry and haul to the stack, the heads of the ears of corn have been known to start sprouting, unable to thrash or sell it, finishing up only good enough for bedding or if it is oats feeding to the cattle.

In the post war year's, teams of Polish and German prisoners of war were drafted onto the farms to help with the harvesting. They were very dedicated and hard working, and when required, were set the task of stooking the corn. Dad would often comment on the speed and quality of their work, saying that if you were to point a gun up the row of stooks, and because they were stooked in such a straight row the bullet would come out at the other end of the field without touching the side of the last stook.

As the corn binder got nearer the centre of the field, and the standing corn became narrower, the activity of the workers would noticeably change. Knowing that we were cutting corn, members of the local game keeping paternity, with their guns and dogs together with farming friends and other local folk with stiff walking sticks, would congregate into the field, As the binder drew to the last few lines of standing corn, the friends would encircle the field close to where the binder was passing, looking into the standing corn with great anticipation. Farms were over-run by rabbits and foxes, so, some had been driven by the binder into the centre of the standing corn, waiting for the moment to attempt an escape. The driver of the tractor as he rode along the edge of the corn would occasionally stand up and start pointing into the standing corn to indicate where the animals were. Before long, folks would be shouting frantically, and signalling at one another, as the rabbits started to emerge. Then the sticks would start to be wielded, as the guns started going off and the dogs started to run in all directions collecting the kill. This excitement would continue for some time until the last line of standing corn was cut. Then the tractor and binder and everybody in the field would suddenly go quiet, while the last dead rabbits were being collected to where the kill was proudly displayed.

Loading the dray with the sheaves was an art, layering the first sheaves around the edge of the bed with the ears facing inwards, then the next circle overlapping the first by half a length, working towards the centre of the dray, then recommencing on the outside again for the next layer. Nearing the top of the load you would start to bring the outer laying a few inches inwards to narrow off like the roof of a house, completing the load after three or four more layers.

The majority of the crop would be hauled to the Dutch barn, and then when the barn was fully stacked in a rick opposite. If there was not room at the farmstead you would occasionally build a rick in the field. Before commencing to build a freestanding rick, a line of tree trunks, up to seven inches in diameter would be placed along the perimeter of the stack, so as to tilt the sheaves inwards to prevent the stack leaning outwards, and collapsing. A thin layer of spoilt straw would be placed on the ground to prevent the sheaves from getting damp. Although methods change around the country, the technique of stacking the sheaves in the Dutch barn was exactly the same as for loading the dray, but when stacking them in the field a slightly different method was used. You would begin by making a round stook in the centre and building around it, gradually lowing each sheave each time you made the next circle until when you were nearing the edge of the stack the sheaves were lain on their side. Then you started from the outside and worked back in as with the method in the Dutch barn. This was to keep the heads of grain up from getting damp. You needed a good eye to make sure you kept the stack upright and the layers level. When the stack height was beyond the reach of the worker standing on the floor of the dray, an elevator was positioned against the rick, with the dray being drawn alongside it. Most of the workmen could put their hand to any type of work, except tractor driving.

One season Mr. Tom Taylor 'senior' was stacking the rick at the top of the Windmill field, unaware that as he built the stack it was progressively leaning downhill. Without any warning the rick started to move, toppling right over onto its side, totally covering 'Mr' as he was known. Dad hastily ran round the side of the fallen rick, trying to find where 'Mr' was, and calling out "*Mr, are you all right?*" Mr, hastily replied, "*Iye. I be alright, I be yusted to it.*" Mr's stacking was sure telling us that he was *used* to falling with the unstable corn stacks he built.

Once the cornfields were cleared, it was the pride of the farmer to get the fields ploughed as soon as possible. If the field was not being replanted in the autumn, the ploughed field was left over winter for the frost to help break up the soul to minimise cultivation the following spring. Prior to ploughing, during the summer when the cattle were still out living in the fields, before being brought back in for winter, and before fruit picking or root lifting commenced, this was an ideal time to empty the farmyards and give the field a good dressing of farmyard manure. In the days of horses they would fill the two-wheeled cart by hand, hauling it up to the fields and tipping the manure into heaps to be spread across the soil later. It would also give the manure time to rot down, and make the job of spreading the manure much easier as the manure was broken up and lighter to handle. Soon after tractors appeared on the farms, manure spreaders became available. We employed Stuart Skip a local agricultural contractor to spread the manure using tractor drawn spreaders. Each season he hired out to us four manure spreaders together with two tractors and two drivers. We used our own two tractors to tow the other two spreaders which Dad and John drove.

Plate 4:6 Threashing at the barn

Using sturdy four tined manure forks we would load each spreader by hand with a worker working on each side, filling the front first and working to the back. It was hot work and a very favourable way of keeping warm, mainly because the heat being given off from the manure, which was only months old and the straw, which was still full bodied, had not had time to rot down. The manure was like a mat all woven together with the straw needing to be dragged apart up, anything up to three feet deep. The smell was acceptably pleasant, and after a mornings work you developed the added bonus of a good appetite.

60

The manure spreader was a long narrow trailer with high wooden sides. Along the floor, ran a conveyor chain with metal cross members to push the manure to the rear, driven by the two large wheels at the rear of the spreader. At the rear opening across the width of the spreader were two large shafts, each having a double row of steel blades sticking out, rotating inwards in opposite directions, chopped the manure into manageable sized pieces as it was pushed backwards. The chopped manure immediately encountered the side of a screw shaped auger, which slung the manure backwards spreading it out across the field.

One damp season, to prevent the fields from becoming rutted the tractors were taking loaded manure spreaders in a spread out convoy along the main Bromyard road, which ran around the outskirts of the farm up to the Bringsty fields. Once unloaded, travelling in a one-way circuit they then came back down the shorter route, through the big Gaines wood, which was on the edge of the farm, and through Stoney Foot orchard, because taking the loaded trailers up the steep orchard would have cut up the field, and travelling through the wood, along the narrow track, would be difficult for the spreaders and tractors to pass.

One of the villagers, on seeing this constant stream of tractors and loaded manure spreaders only passing one way, stopped one of the tractor drivers, and asked, *"Where are you going with these tractors, because I have not seen any of you come back?"*. The driver soon explained the mystery.

In later years, we hired Watkins and Griffith to do the manure hauling. He had purchased a Manure Lift Fork, which fitted on the three-point linkage at the rear of a Fordson Diesel Major tractor. This tractor, always driven by Tom Watkins accompanied the team of manure spreaders.

It was an impressive site to watch him manoeuvring the tractor and fork to load the manure spreaders. With the throttle of the engine well out, and the tractor in high ratio reverse he would surge backwards with the fork rubbing the floor thrusting it into the pile of manure. He would allow the wheels to continue turning often-releasing clouds of smoke from the tyres. Then pulling hard on the forklift leaver, instead of the fork lifting the manure, and because of the weight of manure it was trying to lift, the front wheels would surge up to 5 feet into the air. While Tom stayed unperturbed, and the rear wheels still turning, the tractor would

61

gain more weight onto the rear wheels and would thrust rearwards with the full fork suddenly rising out of the manure, in time with the front wheels hitting the ground with a distinct thud.

The moment the front wheels hit the ground he would throw the tractor into forward gear, at the same time pressing his foot firmly onto one of the independent rear wheel foot brakes, swinging the tractor round on the spot, often with the weight of the fork now swinging high in the air, causing the tractor front wheels to rise again.

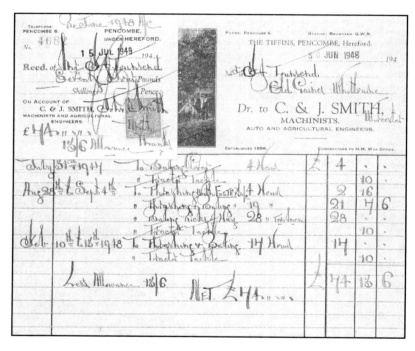

Plate 4:7 Invoice for threshing corn

No sooner had he swung the tractor round he would thrust it back into reverse shooting across the shed, coming to an abrupt halt with the fork sitting midway over the centre of the spreader. He immediately pulled a lever behind his seat, which allowed the fork to tip and let the manure out. Once the manure was discharge the fork was so balanced to cause it to swing shut. Before the fork had gone click Tom would have thrust the tractor back into forward gear, pacing towards the centre of the yard, thrusting his foot on one of the rear wheel brakes to swing the tractor around on the spot, crashing the gearbox into reverse to begin the next fork full.

While all this was happening, one of the other drivers would come rumbling down the yard, with engine in full flight, abruptly stopping. He would jump off, and onto the tractor with the loaded spreader, moving it out of the way and replace it with the empty one, and off to go again.

At the onset of autumn when all the planting and fruit picking was done, then threshing the corn could commence. It was always exciting to wake up one morning, while still in bed to hear the unusual throb of a large tractor engine, and the metallic sound of iron wagon wheels coming up the lane. Looking through the window we gazed at the large orange Case tractor slowly drawing a large orange threshing box, neatly covered with a green tarpaulin, towing a stationary bailer and a green labourers living caravan. Because of the length of the thrashing equipment being towed, the tractor was not able to drive straight into the farm drive. Jack Smith hired out the set of threshing tack, driven by George Baynham who was in charge of the threshing kit. First the bailer and Living Caravan were unhitched from the threshing box, and the threshing box towed just into the farm entrance and parked. The bailer and caravan were then towed farther along the side of the drive entrance, where the caravan would be unhitched and stay for the duration of the threshing. Frank the labourer, travelled with the thrashing tack, as it was termed, and lived in the caravan. Franks caravan was typical of the caravans used by shepherds in bleaker parts of England and Wales during lambing time. Its furnishings were very basic comprising a bunk bed, with storage space underneath. The caravan also had a little cast iron stove, fed with wood or coal, accompanied on top by a small well-coated black chard kettle. Frank would occasionally invite me in for a cup of tea, to taste the warm, cosy homely comfort. After adding water to the kettle he would draw it over the centre of the stove, and after giving the stove coals a gentle stir with a poker, wait a long while for it to come to the boil. While it was coming to the boil, he would add another spoon of tea, together with milk and sugar into the teapot, and eventually pore in more hot water, topping up the water from the previous brew. When he poured the tea out, it was nearly black, and well strong to drink. On many occasions, Frank was heard asking George if he would like to join him for a cup of tea, but George, knowing the strength of Frank's brew always managed to find a way out of having to except the invitation.

The baler was then taken on into the rick yard and parked in its approximate working position. The threshing box was now towed into its final position behind the baler. The tractor used to drive the equipment would be driven behind the threshing box on the opposite side to the baler. The difficult part of setting up the three pieces of equipment was about to begin. The threshing box and baler and the tractor had to be manoeuvred to get all three lined up in a straight and level line, for if there was the slightest misalignment, the drive belts would jump off their pulleys. It would also enable the sheaves of corn passing through the thrashing drums to stay central and on the level, evening out the threshing operation. This would include the use of jacks, wooden blocks and a built in spirit level fitted onto the threshing box. From the tractor a conveyor belt, set at the right tension drove the threshing box, and then a belt from the same shaft on the threshing box drove the baler.

Early next morning we were awakened by the endearing and distinct sound of yum-yum-yum-more-more-more of the threshing drums, as the full set of threshing machinery sprang into life, together with the hum of the chaff fans which blow the chaff across the rickyard into a heap, through a 7" diameter tube, held horizontal by a pair of crossed wooden support legs. Then you would hear the threshing machine start to groan each time Frank, with meticulous rhythm, fed the sheaves into the drum on top of the threshing box. Catching a sheaf by the forefinger of his left hand, he then took his razor sharp knife held in his right hand and hooked the end under the string, and with a sharp tug cut the string releasing the sheaf, dropping it into the hopper, retaining the strings in his left hand, for use to tie the sacks of corn. Two workmen would be lined up on top of the rick feeding the sheaves to Frank.

In time with the hum of the thrashing machine you would hear the rattle of the box shaped ram inside the baler rolling to and fro along on its trolley, with a distinct thump, as it came to the end of the track hitting against the compressed straw, in tune with the nodding horses head popping up and down as it pushed the loose straw into the heart of the baler.

It was at the other end of the threshing box that the thrashed corn entered the sacks. A large barn door had been laid on the ground, to prevent the sacks from getting muddy and wet. Jack would be busy, unhooking the full sacks and exchanging them with empty ones. If it was oats being thrashed he would detach the bags from the thrasher, and roll the well full Godsell Brown bags, (which could weigh up to 2.1/4 cwt if used for wheat), onto a sack lift. The sack lift had a handle on the side that turned a shaft attached to two chains hooked to a platform on the floor. Jack would wind the handle, raising the platform with the bag on it, till the bag was high enough for him to lay it over his shoulders and carry it into the tractor barn close by. Wheat and barley would be carried in smaller 1 cwt sacks. Meanwhile George would spend most of his time feeding the wires through the side of the baler chamber, trotting around the other side to tie them, stacking them as they fell off the discharge end of the baler. The rest of his time was spent greasing, oiling bearings, or holding a lump of wax against the belts to improve their grip.

When the height of the rick reaches only three or four feet from the ground, the farm dogs would be let loose, and extra helpers drafted in with sticks or spades. Suddenly rats and mice would dart out from the base of the rick, and run in all directions. The workers would start shouting to draw attention to the dogs to where the vermin were escaping from, while their spades and stick would start to swing in all directions. The dogs would dart here and there, catching the rats by the neck, and with a sharp shake break its neck leaving it on the ground to dash after another it has spotted. If one of the dogs favoured catching mice, he would swallow them whole until he was full, disappear into a corner, and regurgitate them, then recommence the hunt.

One Dutch barn bay would take a full day to thresh, so after a well-earned tea break, the laborious task of resighting the machinery against the next bay would begin in readiness to start threshing early the next day.

With the help of the neighbouring farmer in the early years, Dad would have a barrel of cider brewed, for the threshing team to drink, which sat on a wooden platform in the woodshed. One season, soon after the first tea/cider break, he noticed the workmen were getting noisy and very merry. On inspection of the cider barrel and one whiff of the contents, he discovered the cider had been put into a perry barrel. The combination had increased the alcohol content, making it exceptionally potent. Dad immediately pulled the plug and let the contents flow into the Lake, never to repeat the good will gesture again. My only memory of the event is going to the woodshed seeing the empty barrel, putting my nose to the plughole on the top side of the barrel and taking a quick sniff for myself.

Once the threshing was complete the wheat corn was sold onto the local grain merchant, J. W. Williams from Bromyard who would be responsible for collecting it. If there was any damp found in the bags of wheat, it needed to be collected immediately, for the corn merchant to put it through their corn dryer. Mr. Fee, the merchant's representative negotiated the sale price of the corn with Dad, taking into consideration the cost of drying, unfortunately lowering the profits on the corn for that season.

The oat corn was transported by dray or cart, from the tractor shed and emptied onto the granary floor over the cowshed, to a depth of two feet. In an inclement season the oats may still be damp, so it would need turning regularly, to prevent it going mouldy, and congealing into solid damp lumps. Turning was carried out by clambering over the grain wearing wellingtons to stop the grain getting into your shoes, and drawing the manure slurry scraper though the grain or, using a large grain shovel turn the whole area over by hand to let the air circulate through. As winter progressed Jack would start to bag up the oats into small wheat bags, and with the aid of the sack lifter hoist them onto his back, and carry the bags to the bottom barn to grind up for animal feed. It was much easier for two to fill the bags, with one holding the bad top open while the other shovelled the corn in, but I found the bagging up very unpleasant. In the centre of the entrance door, about 5" up from the base and 6" in diameter was a hole for the cats to get in, to help keep the mice and rats down. The cats found the grain a very easy toilet area, so a small shovel was always at hand to flip the smelly deposits through the doorway into the top cattle yard, before bagging up commenced.

Jack Smith, who we hired the threshing machinery from, introduced us to the first Combine Harvesters. The combined wheat grain and the stalks would ripen together, so it could be

66

combined as soon as it was ripe, whereas when the oat grains were ripe, the stems took up to a further fortnight to dry. So to prevent the moisture passing into the grain when harvesting, you had to wait until the stalks were dry first, making for some difficulties in an inclement season. One of the first models of Combine that came onto the farm was the Massey Harris, which had a single wheel on the back used for steering. This first model was driven by George, who when he reached the end of each cut, found great delighted in stopping abruptly, throwing the machine into reverse, and wanting to speedily turn back into the next cut, would swing the steering wheel round 180 Deg., quickly letting the clutch out, swinging the rear end of the combine harvester round in reverse on the spot, throwing the bag handlers on top of the machine unexpectedly onto the side rail, who then spent some few moments gaining composure trying to find their balance. The combine performed well, but there was one dangerous drawback. The petrol engine was positioned low down, underneath in the centre the machine, and got a liberal covering of dust and chaff. Hardly a season passed without hearing that a Massey Harris combine had gone on fire destroying the field of corn with it.

When Jack Smith gave up his Agricultural Contracting business Watkins and Griffith came to cut our corn using a Claas combine harvester. This machine had a Ford diesel engine mounted on the top of the combine harvester, greatly reducing the risk of fire. The only other risk of a combine harvester catching fire was if a bearing became dry through lack of lubrication and the friction caused it to get red hot, causing the dust and chaff to catch light.

Early combine harvesters needed two additional workers standing on a platform behind the driver to bag up the corn. The threshed grain was conveyed up into a container on the top of the machine, which graded the corn, and then channelled the corn down through four funnels into the sacks. As the sacks rapidly filled one worker would be busy removing and tying the tops, while his mate replaced another empty one. Once the top of the sack was tied, with the workers back lent heavy against the safety rail to keep his balance, he would haul the base of the sack round and onto an angular metal trough acting as a chute allowing the sack to slide down, hitting a strong spring loaded metal gate at the bottom, just a few inches off the ground. When the combine got near to the field gate, one of the workers would pull a rope alongside the chute, and allow all the bags to slide onto the ground to await the tractor and trailer to collect them and take them back to the farmstead.

Later because of rising labour costs and wider cutter bars the combines were designed with a large tank that discharged the corn direct into a trailer, via an auger. This meant change to our storage facility. We had to get a silo erected, and add a second set of sideboards to the trailers to transport the corn. In an inclement season if the corn was not quite dry especially the wheat, we would have to transport the corn by trailer straight to the merchant in Bromyard, where it could be dried immediately.

Chapter 5

Fruit Picking

Walking through the orchards in the late autumn, you would see small piles of twigs, and branches laying on the ground around the trees. Jack, tall slim with large strong rugged hands, wearing navy blue dungarees, would be seen with a long handled pruner, reaching up into the centre of the trees lopping off the new growth on the inner of the lower boughs, which would have taken up precious energy on next years crop, needed for growth on the outer branches, where the best fruit grew. Later with a ladder gently laid into the branches, and with a small pruning saw in the right hand, he would lop off any dangerous dead branches. When finished, he would collect the smaller twigs or branches, and tie them into small bundles called faggots. The faggots would be carried home and used for kindling or as starting wood for the farmhouse fire in winter, with the more sturdy branches being sawn up into logs.

My early experience of fruit growing was being taken by Dad to the Stoney Foot orchard, carrying with him a pruning saw, a Tilley lamp, a small tin of tar paint and brush, a reel of raffia, together with a quantity of cuttings or saplings. The apple cuttings were purchased from the fruit merchant, and the pear saplings were freshly cut from one of the other pear trees in the orchard. The purpose was to replace certain trees with other species of apples and pears that were more marketable. He would select a tree of medium age; saw through all the prime branches two to three feet from the main trunk. With a very sharp penknife he would carefully cut a slit 3 inches long, from the saw cut along the length of the trunk, just under the bark, gently prising the bark open. Selecting one of the saplings, he would cut away its bark from the base to the equivalent length of the slit in the branch, then cut away half of the thickness of the stem, He then slid the sapling gently down inside the bark, with the outer diameter of the sapling against the inner side of the bark of the branch. More than one graft would be made to each branch in case one did not take. He would liberally rap the raffia around the full length of the graft till it was totally hidden. At the start of the job the Tilley would have been lit, with the tin of tar paint sitting on the top. By now the paint would have well melted, so a generous amount was painted onto the saw cut on the end of the branch to keep out the rain and any disease getting in.

In spring once the fruit has set, and the petals had fallen, the trees were sprayed against fungus, disease and pests. We had acquired an ex-army trailer to carry a 500-gallon tank, and a twin piston pump attached to a petrol engine. Two pressure hoses would be attached to the pump. On the end of each hose was a long brass tube of 6-foot length with an on/off lever at the connection, and a control jet on the other end. You could easily reach all the branches from the ground by using the tubular extensions.

Having finished harvesting, having emptied the yards of the manure onto the ground, having ploughed the manure in, and with the winter corn planted, it would be late September. The damsons would be ready for picking. Following close behind, the plums would be ready, by which time the apples were ready to pick. By the early 1950's we had purchased two twin wheeled three ton tipper trailers. One of the trailers, less side boards would be taken down and drawn alongside the granary, to collect the ladders and fruit baskets.

Grandad Davis had made most of the ladders, being a wheelwright. He would visit the local wood yard and select straight poles of Scotch pine, imported especially for ladder making. The wood merchant would saw the pole in half. Walking the hedgerows he would collect any broken pieces from old wooden gates, and roughly carve them into unfinished rungs. The side members were then marked out and drilled using a tapered reamer to suit the tapered ends of the rungs. He calculated precisely the length of each rung, to get the correct taper along the length of the ladder. Each rung was carefully cut to fit each hole on the side members. The rungs were fitted to the one side member and then the two sides were brought together. The local blacksmith would forge the feet, and a bolt or long stud fitted under every other rung, cut from a length of roding with a thread on each end cut with a die. The ladders were stored along and in between the cross beams of the granary, above the loose grain of oats, with the picking baskets hanging from them. They would be gently slid out from between the beams and placed one on top of another along the length of the trailer, with the foot of the ladders placed over the front vertical screw mechanism for tipping the trailer, as a support. The ladders would be roped on at the rear end, and the baskets hung by their hooks dangling from the rear. The trailer would then move to the top barn to load the fruit boxes, used to carry 48 lbs of damsons and 40lb for pears, plums and apples, delivered by the fruit merchant some days previous.

Plate 5:1 Jack Burriston and Jim Overton

Once in the orchard the ladders needed unloading with care, because they could easily be broken. When not in use, the ladders should be placed sideways against a tree on the ground to be easily seen, to prevent getting run over by the tractor. The grass by now would be quite long. It was unwise to allow any animals into the orchard to graze, because the cattle could choke on a small apple, but also their dropping would foul up any fruit on the floor awaiting to be collected later for cider making. You needed to be strong and have a steady hand to lift the ladders and place them into the trees. Laying the ladder on its side against your leg you needed to stand just above half way along facing towards its base, so the main of the weight is on the lower end of the ladder. Then keeping the ladder in the sideways position, taking the topside of the ladder with both hands, you lifted it up and placed the lower side onto your right shoulder. Next you would lean slightly forward, to drive the spikes at the base of the ladder firmly into the ground, and begin to walk towards the base, while the side of the ladder slid up your shoulder, rising vertically into the air, till it was totally upright. Then drawing your right hand round and under the ladder, clasping and reaching a rung at the most comfortable position below, then with the other hand reaching and clasping a rung with your left hand above as far as you can comfortably reach, lift the ladder straight up vertically, and begin to carry it towards the tree. If it is one of the large ladders, with 40 rungs and 30 feet in length, and because of its weight and difficulty to balance you would lower the ladder spikes into the ground, holding it vertically for a few moments, to allow you time to decide where to place the ladder in the tree for the safest position. You would always select a branch that has a sturdy division of outer branches to lower the ladder into. You would also ensure the ladder is placed towards the centre of the tree, so if the branch were to break, the ladder would only end up in the centre, bringing you little harm.

You need to be agile and nimble as well as having a good head for heights together with a degree of confidence to climb and manoeuvre on ladders. There are times, when you see that perfectly shaped apple which is sitting right on the farthest point of a twig. You have to lean out with one hand anchored to the rung of the ladder, with your weight helping to balance the ladder, taking the strain to the limit, without both you and the ladder twisting or being pulled sideways and coming out of the tree.

As well as ensuring you pick a suitable ladder for the tree there is an art to picking fruit. Damson trees are a good introduction to fruit picking, as they do not grow very large, so you will only need a 15 to 20-rung ladder. The fruit is easy to pick, but you must ensure you do not pick the fruit with the stalk on, and make sure you do not include leaves, to avoid a reprimand from the farmer. Pears have to be picked with their stalks on, but if the trees are not replaced before they get very old, they will, like apple trees have branches reaching straight up into the heaven's, and because of the often slender and sparse nature of the branches, require the longest of ladders, needing great confidence and skill, where to place the ladder, becoming a very precarious operation. Having to climb to the top of a tall tree where the ladder is only propped by the top branches of the tree, calls for extra support to prevent the ladder

72

springing as you climb. A pair of props, made from a couple of hazel poles, with a fork at the top, would be placed diagonally, up against the rungs, with feet splayed out, behind the ladder to create a rigid triangle and much needed support. Plums are picked easily without their stalks on, but apples have strong stalks and require a full twist with the wrist to part them from the twigs.

Our orchards covered about 25 acres. The majority of them were bramley-cooking apples and cider apples. Together with a few eating apples there was quite a large number of pear trees, including damson and plum trees.

As it was autumn the afternoon daylight would come down quickly, so by mid-afternoon it was time to load the full boxes of apples onto the trailer, and get them back to the farm before it was totally dark. The bramley's were tipped onto the top barn floor, on a mat of straw, but all the other fruit would stay in their boxes. Dad would spend his evenings sorting, grading and weighing the apples and pears, for the merchant to collect the following evening, to free up much needed space for the next picking. The damsons and plums just needed weighing. It was very difficult to pass the top barn at any time of autumn and winter, when there was fruit stored in them. The aroma of the fruit was so inviting, that each time you walked up the drive passed the barn, you succumbed to going in and picking up either a Cox's Pippin eating apple or a Conference pear to give you some appetising refreshment. There were not sufficient plums to sell, so mum would collect the plums from the barn, and take them to the kitchen, either boiling them to store in bottles or make jam. The cider apples were left till last. Jack would take to the orchard a long pole with a hook on the end and start to shake the branches to dislodge the apples. We would employ the same group of women folk who helped with the potato picking, to collect the apples into buckets and tip them into hession sacks. Although these were the same sacks as were used for corn, and had got a few small holes in them, the apple bags needed to be stored separately after each season, because the apple juice would contaminate the bags, making them smell, and would very quickly rot them, if they were not dried after use. Once there were a sufficient number of bags filled, we would inform the haulage company to collect the bags, and transport them to the cider processing plant at Bulmer's in Hereford. On arrival the driver would have the entire load weighed including the lorry. Then after emptying the sacks by hand before leaving the factory, the lorry was weighed again, receiving a ticket giving the tare weight of the fruit, returning back to the farm to drop off the empty bags.

At the end of the 1950's Britain joined the Common Market, with large quantities of fruit being imported in from Europe. Britain could not compete with the quality of imported fruit so the government encouraged farmers to uproot all their orchards by offering them grants. Seeing the way the fruit farming industry was moving Dad applied for a grant, rooting up most of the trees, but just keeping a few damson, plum and pear trees for the farmhouse. Work started in May to uproot the trees in the Stoney Foot orchard, the part of the season between planting roots and before haymaking commenced. Dad used the Field Marshal tractor to uproot the trees for it had very good traction enhanced by both rear wheels being filled with water. By tying a steel rope firmly to the top of the tree trunk or round some of the larger lower branches, the Field Marshal made little work of pulling the trees over. The process of tree felling, could be seen and heard for some distance away, with the large exhaust of the tractor throwing out intermittent plumes of diesel smoke into the sky in time with the upper branches waving to and fro, resisting to being felled. Combined with the high pitched squeal of the clutch being released and pressed, and the surge of the engine, frequently increasing in speed to the loud futt-futt-futt of the engine, with the tractor lurching forward and backwards, she would dig herself in to the soil with the back wheels creating large deep ruts. Then hearing the sound of cracking as the roots gave way suddenly, the front of the tractor would give a final leap forward up into the air, as the rear of the tractor lurched forward out of the ruts, with the tree finally falling to the ground. In the early days of the project once the trees were felled, we lopped off all the branches from the trunk, with axes, into cord lengths (that is a standard length for fire wood of about four feet long) and burnt up all the smaller branches and twigs. A school friend of mine often came and helped me, during holidays, and evenings, as he was very interested in taking up forestry, when he left school. We often engaged in the logger's technique of working on a big branch together. You would stand either side of the branch, and take it in turns to wield the axe, in rhythm, cleaving out a vee shape, working our way through the branch. If either of you got your axe stuck, you had to be very quick to hold fire, for it was at the moment that one was about to bring his axe down.

I was now old enough to drive the tractors around the farm. One day I was driving the Field Marshal across the slope of the orchard steering my way between the fallen trees and turning the front wheels to miss the open holes from where the roots had been torn out. My friend Roger was sitting with his bottom overhanging the rear mudguard of the tractor; swaying back and forward as the tractor occasionally dipped into a shallow root hole. Unfortunately, I managed to loosen my grip from the tractor steering wheel for a moment and let the tractor dip into a deeper and larger than normal hole, on the side Roger was sitting, which had large jagged roots left sticking out from the side. Roger was instantly thrown backward towards the hole by the motion of the tractor, then instantly leaned forwards to keep his balance to the loud bang and the whoosh of water spraying up from the outer side of the rear tyre, surging up into the sky, well wetting Rogers's backside and shirt. The jagged root had caught the valve tearing it from the inner tube, releasing all the ballast water out. While my friend walked home to change his clothes, I had to walk back to the farm in trepidation to tell dad what had happened. But much to my relief, without even making any remarks he immediately rang J. C. Baker, the Worcester Agricultural Machinery dealer to come and repair the tyre. The root in the hole had snapped off the valve to the inner tube, so thankfully it only meant a new inner tube, and the tyre being refilled with water, and the necessary additive to prevent the water freezing in winter.

Cutting the twelve-inch trunks and sturdy branches with axes soon became a long hard chore. Chain saws at this time were only just coming into circulation, with most models only able to work in the upright position. So we hired two chain saws with operators, greatly speeding up the work. Most of the tree trunks were of sufficient size to be lifted by two onto the trailers. If they were over a foot in diameter you would split the trunk in half. With the sharp edge of an axe, you would make a split at one end and then drive a steel cleat in by a 12lb. sledgehammer. Because the wood was freshly cut with the sap still moist the trunk would readily split in half. All the cordwood, of about four feet in length was then transported to the rickyard to clear the orchard for ploughing, ready to be cut up by circular saw at a later date.

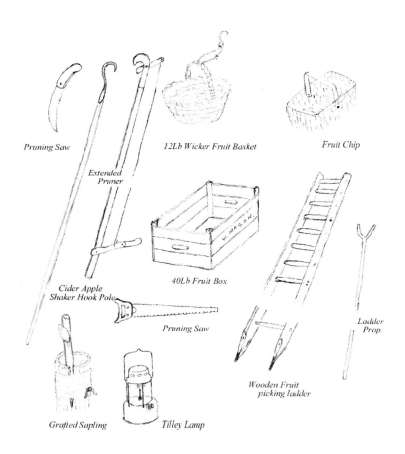

Pruning Saw

12Lb Wicker Fruit Basket

Fruit Chip

Extended
Pruner

Cider Apple
Shaker Hook Pole

40Lb Fruit Box

Pruning Saw

Ladder
Prop.

Wooden Fruit
picking ladder

Grafted Sapling

Tilley Lamp

Plate 5:2 Tools for fruit growing

The trees need annual pruning, and new grafts to give better stocks.
When picking in tall trees the ladder needs a pair of props for support.
The hook pole is for shaking off the apples used for cider making.

76

Burning the apple wood produced a very sweet aroma, but has nothing to compare with the rich odours of pear wood. The logs Pear wood are so easy to split with an axe, either dry or when the sap is rising.

Attempting to plough the orchards with the trailer plough behind the Field Marshal would have caused a lot of frustration. There were many large roots still left in the ground, so you would have been constantly stopping and re-coupling the plough to the automatic spring trip, which would trip every time you hit a large stone or wedged under a root. Because most of the orchards were very steep, it meant they could be only ploughed down hill one way, and meant making difficult turning manoeuvres at the bottom and returning slowly again to the top. Dad asked Watkins and Griffith the local Agricultural Contractors to help by bringing along their three-point link, three furrow, hydraulic mounted plough, which could easily be lifted out of the ground if it got wedged under a root. Once lifted out of the ground at the end of the field the tractor could reverse back up with its rear wheel in the last turned furrow at a much greater rate than the Field Marshal towing the trailer plough.

Stan one of the partners in the contractors business brought along a three-furrow plough with one of the first four-wheel drive Fordson Major diesel tractors bought second hand. Stan drove the tractor with great confidence and agility, impressing Dad with its powerful traction and agility. It was most impressive when climbing the steep banks as well as the speed of reversing, particularly when having to plough the orchards one way. As I watched Stan driving the tractor, I became particularly impressed with the traction they had and developed a very fond liking to four-wheel drive vehicles. It made a lasting impression upon me, creating in me the desire to own a four-wheel drive vehicle of my own when old enough to drive. Dad using the Field Marshal then crossed the ploughed orchards towing the Cambridge roll to flatten the furrows and break down the clods. It was very precarious as you waddled across the furrows, along the slopes, towing the roll. Following behind with the Fordson Major E27N John would then use the disc harrows to get a suitable tilth for planting. Some of the orchards were planted with corn, and then finally planted down with grass seed. For one or two seasons the Stoney Foot Orchard was planted with Kale. Kale is a member of the cabbage family, growing up to 4 feet 6 inches high, with cabbage like leaves growing most of the way up a sturdy stem similar to a brussel sprout stalk. The kale controlled by strip grazing was for feeding the dairy cows in winter. Strip grazing is using an electric fence to allow the animals to eat only a short strip of plants like grass, kale, turnips, to prevent them from over indulging and spoiling the rest of the crop by treading it into the soil. Each morning before turning the cows out from milking Dad would send me out to move the electric fence. Using a long handled hedge bill or hook you cut a walkway of about two feet wide, leaving a strip of standing kale about four feet in width, for the cattle to graze. On a frosty morning, particularly if there had been any rain a day or two earlier, the kale would be covered in attractive icicles. I needed to dress up well, ensuring the collar of my jacket was well up to cover my neck, wearing a pair of gauntlet gloves to protect my hands and arms, and of course as always wearing wellingtons. As I thrashed the kale with the billhook the bitter cold icicles would fly everywhere, landing down around my neck, behind the gauntlet of my gloves, and down the inside of my wellingtons as well as giving my face a good burning. Then after switching off the electric, and untying the electric fence wire from the posts spaced every five or six yards apart, I swung the wire over the kale into the walkway. The metal posts had rubber insulators on the top where, once in position, you re-threaded the wire through. At each end was an extra sturdy post with an angular support. One end had a small winch to tension the wire, which once tensioned you could switch the electric back on, giving out the distinctive tick- tick, as the power pulsed out twice every second.

All the fruit trees on the farm, except the Hollow Orchard were lifted using the Field Marshal. To speed up the work, the last two orchards the Drive orchard and Hollow Orchard, the contractors used a crawler to push the trees over, cutting down on time and effort. In the Drive orchard there were some stumps of very large oak, hornbeam and sycamore trees, the left overs from trees sold for furniture making. Dad needed to uproot them to save having to manoeuvre round them when cultivating the ground. So the contractors brought a JCB with a homemade cutter attached to the end of the jib. The cutter was like a quarter section of a circular saw blade with four or five hardened teeth welded on the circumference. Using the arm of the JCB and hydraulics to pitch the blade it would slice into the ground along side the tree trunk, cutting through all the roots. Once the driver had cut through the roots of the stumps, he then turned the tractor round and with a gentle nudge of the raised front bucket pushed the tree over. The following summer after reseeding one of the smaller orchards down to grass, we noticed poppies growing in great numbers in amongst the freshly sown young grass. It was an amazing sight and quite unique for poppies never grew again in that orchard. These seeds must have laid dormant in the ground to wait for the right conditions to germinate. Poppies are annuals so with cutting the grass before the seeds had ripened, most probably prevented them growing again. Later in the season in the same orchard we had another surprise. Towards the end of September, if we have had a warm, dry summer and then we have a few days of warm rain, there is the chance to see a few mushrooms growing on some of the pastureland, particularly where sheep have been grazing. This orchard just for one season grew an enormous amount of mushrooms, producing up to two fruit baskets full each day.

I miss the community spirit and pleasure of taking a ladder, to pick a few damsons, pears or apples for home use, and the aroma they give off, which adds to the atmosphere and comforts of farm life.

Chapter 6

Shepherding

Although Dad's care of the animals was excellent, showing much care and empathy, there were times when he had to make hard decisions, especially when dealing with animals that were sick or terminally ill. All the animals on the farm would be visited daily, by someone, whether they needed feeding or not, whether at the farmstead or in the fields. Dad took personal responsibility for the sheep. Every day he would take one of the two black and white sheep dogs with him. On average we kept about one hundred sheep, mainly Cheviots, and a few Cluns together with two Suffolk rams, or tups as they were more often called. Both sheep dogs Toss and Sam were kept tied up in the bottom barn, alongside where the animal feed was mixed. Sam the younger of the sheep dogs was tethered by the large double barn doors facing the farmhouse. During day light hours he would spend his time laid flat on all fours with his lower jaw laid on the floor between his front legs, and his eyes glued to the farmhouse back door.

It did not matter what time of day you left the farmhouse, having decided to visit the sheep, he knew instantly and would immediately stand up and pull frantically on his chain, his tongue hanging out, and frantically wagging his tail. As you approached the barn door, Sam would be pent up with excitement, choking himself on his chain trying to hang himself, impatiently waiting for me to unhook him. His front feet would be pouncing up and down off the floor, his tongue dangly happily out his mouth showing his shiny white teeth, grinning from ear to ear and his tail wagging wildly. Sam had the uncanny knowledge of where he was going.

The rear of the barn had a pair of wide double doors with a gap of fifteen inches from the floor, which invariably were open. Along the ground to fill the gap was a two-foot high board to stop the smaller animals and hens from coming in to the barn and helping themselves to all the grain used for feeding. On releasing Sam from his chain, in two short leaps he was over the board, and darted straight up to the next gate that leads into the farm drive. He would stand with his nose tight to the gap where the gate fastened, waiting for me to catch up. Patiently waiting together with his ears pulled back with heart racing and lungs panting, and his tongue hanging out, his eyes glistening and smiling, as his eyes glanced to and fro keeping one eye on you, you sensed him saying hurry up and get *that* gate opened! The moment the gate was opened he would race up the full length of the drive to the road, and loiter by the entrance sniffing and watering the gateposts, waiting till I had caught up, and then dutifully walk alongside me up to the field.

Plate 6:1   Cheviot and Clun ewes with young lambs

Once we were inside the field with the sheep I had to vigilantly keep Sam at my side, for again he would be on full alert waiting for instructions. With the command *"Get by."*, at the moment I raise my arm and pointed my hand in a certain direction, he was off like a thunder bolt, with his legs striding out till his stomach was almost touching the ground, racing around the edge of the field to gather the sheep together, and draw the flock towards where I was standing. Sam when young was over enthusiastic so you had to be very firm with your commands of *"Back   Stay – Stay!."*. Once the sheep were together you had to shout, *"Sit!"* perhaps more than once, till he had used up some of his energy. When all the sheep had gathered around you and both sheep and dog had settled down for a few moments, you would ask the dog to gently drive the sheep between you and the hedge allowing the sheep to walk single file past you to count them. Occasionally while trying to concentrate on counting, some would sneak behind you, so you would have to send the dog off to collect the escapees to re-group and start the count again.

When I was in my mid-teens, Dad started up in dairying, which took up a lot of his time, so I was privileged to take a larger part in looking after the sheep.

One day as I was on my way up the farm driveway, accompanied by Sam on my way up to count the sheep, a salesman friend of ours from Birmingham, drove into the driveway, and asked "*Where are you going David*?". I replied, "*To count the sheep*". He immediately asked if he could come too, to which I replied "*Yes but its very wet, have you got some wellingtons?*". "*That does not matter*", was his reply, as he parked up his car and stepped into the damp muddy drive with his shining black shoes, and smart black suit. We walked up the lane, and on arriving at the Dipwood field gateway, I suggested he stood and looked over the gate, because the field was so muddy, but no, he wanted to come in, for he wanted to be in on what I was doing. During the previous few days we had had a large amount of rain. The sheep's feet had dug into the wet soil, cutting it up with their footmarks, with the rain filling them with little puddles of water. Our friend tried to pick his way, sprawling his legs out from side to side, trying to avoid the puddles, but each step he took, the clay brown slurry would spray up his trouser legs, totally changing the face of his shoes. Thankfully returning back to the farm and standing for a short while in front of the farmhouse fire the trousers and shoes soon dried off. With a shoe brush and some polish together with a stiff clothes brush, he quickly removed all the soil.

As Autumn grew closer it was time to think of putting the ewes to the rams for mating, so during October the sheep were brought down to the farmstead, and housed in a set of three wooden catching pens, nestled neatly between the Implement shed along side the top end of the farm drive and between a row of elm trees which ran alongside the farm pond. This part of the drive was near to the road and could be gated off to secure the sheep. Alongside the drive and opposite the barn was a fence separating the drive from a paddock, where any of the sheep could be separated, or pasture over night. Not all the sheep could be housed in the first pen, because Dad and John needed working space. So while the majority of the sheep stayed on the drive some were driven into the first pen, onto one rail of the fence. In the second pen, Dad and John attached a sturdy piece of rope tied into a loop, acquired from the outer packing belonging to the reels of baler twine. Dad and John would each catch a sheep, and lead them into the second pen coaxing their heads through the loop of rope, then gently press one leg against the sheep's rear thigh, or rump pinned against the fence to keep her head firmly in the noose of the rope and prevent her from escaping backwards. Taking a pair of sheep daggers or clippers, they would clip away all the wool from around her rump and tail, cutting off any lumps of dry manure, to make them attractive to the two tups, which would soon be joining them. Once the tail trimming was complete you would put one hand under the neck, draw the sheep out from the noose. Then you slipped the other hand across over its back, and under the sheep's stomach, across the udder, and catch hold of the back leg resting against you. Gripping the sheep round its neck firmly with the other arm, you then drew the leg up under the stomach causing the other rear leg to collapse to which the sheep would gently roll back towards you and sit on her rump, with her back lay firmly between you knees. Using a pair of foot trimming clippers you would trim the horny edge of the foot, which had curled into and over each pad, right down until it was level with the middle soft paw. In a wet season, foot rot will set in between the claws and round under the horny edge, so you needed to cut the edge right back to expose the rot in order to add antiseptic and allow the air to get to it, dry it out and aid the healing process. Once all work on the sheep was complete, with one hand under the neck, and one hand on the rump, the sheep would be led into the third pen to keep them separate from the sheep waiting their turn, until all the sheep outside had been attended to.

Lambing had been planned for late spring when the coldest of the winter weather was over, with the two tups being kept separate from the sheep for the summer season. During January to March, the latter weeks of their 21-week pregnancy, especially if it was a hard winter, you would need to supplement their food, to keep them in good health, so as to produce good lambs and a plentiful supply of milk. But it was vital you did not get them too fat, or feed them with mangolds which have a large water content which would bloat the sheep's stomach, bringing there own set of problems. One of the very unpleasant problems you may have to deal with, when the sheep are heavy with lamb is a severe prolapse, commonly termed 'casting the reed'. The sheep will have up to a 4 to 5 inch diameter balloon of the womb, trying to escape out through the uterus. This was a very distressing job to deal with. Dad would take a helper, taking with him a bottle of sedative, some warm water and disinfectant, some soft binder twine and a bagging needle. Once he had caught the ewe, which by now would be quite docile, because of the discomfort, you would first give her a sedative by drenching. This was by simply getting your arm round under her neck, taking a firm hold of the lower jaw and lifting her head up a little. Then the neck of the bottle was slipped down the side of the uplifted jaw inside the mouth and the contents steadily poured into her throat. The bottle was gently tilted up as she swallowed, with the tongue of the sheep moving rapidly in and out as she gently grunted as if to say, "How nice". Meanwhile given a few minutes for the sedative to take effect, dad would wash the exposed womb with water and disinfectant. After laying her on her side he would begin the awesome task of gently pushing the womb back. Threading the bagging needle with the soft string he would break through the skin at the side of the uterus, joining a thread to the other side, putting about four stitches in to prevent the womb re-emerging causing some discomfort to the ewe. From now on you would then keep a wary eye on the ewe to detect when she was about to lamb, so as to cut the stitches to enable her to have a normal birth. In many cases we missed catching the moment when the sheep was about to lamb, but invariable the pressure of the birth would rip the stitches, with no seen discomfort or side effects. The following autumn she would be sent to market with the barren ewes, because if you kept her for another season, it often happened that the same ewe would prolapse again.

Supplementary feed would comprise of a bale or two of nice short sweet lime green hay, together with a sack of oatmeal or a formulated type of protein cake or nuts. Regular feeding would make the sheep very tame, which was a great asset when lambing time arrived. From now on until some time after the lambs are born and ready to wean the dog would stay at home. At feeding time approaching the field gate with a sack over one shoulder the sheep will immediately give out a cry to say the food has arrived and hastily meet you at the gate pushing and bustling, causing you difficulty opening the gate. Then you would make your way to the trough, as their soft coats brush around your legs. You needed to keep a wary eye behind you for if one of the rams manages to get near, they would give you a smart duff up against the back of your knee, with you loosing your balance and suddenly finding yourself sinking to the ground. Alternately the ram would nudge the bottom of the bag and cause you to dislodge it off your shoulder, with the bag falling to the ground, making short work finding the open top and digging his noses deep into it. On most occasions when you have lost your footing some food will have spilt onto the ground, distracting the sheep for sufficient time for you to get the bag back on your shoulder. Arriving at the trough you would gently let the bag roll down onto your right thigh, then taking the open mouth of the bag in the left hand and tucking your other under and around the centre part of the bag, you began to shake a small amount out as you walked along the trough, while the ewes nudged and jostled the back of your ankles to get the first portion falling from the bag.

In mid-March just before lambing commenced the sheep will have been transferred to the Drive Orchard, making the distance to walk a little easier, as you needed to make more frequent visits each day, as the tell tale signs of the first lambs becomes imminent. The sheep will normally keep together while grazing or resting, but you would then notice a sheep isolate herself from the flock, standing close to a hedge or corner of the field, acting in an abnormal way. She would be finding a place suitable to lamb. You would need to keep a frequent eye on the ewe, waiting for up to four hours, before you needed to intervene, for by then it was likely she was in some difficulty.

At the start of the 1960's, Dad had decided to go into dairying. I had now left school and joined Dad on the farm, so, while Dad was busy with milking and feeding twice a day, which means his time was dedicated to the dairy herd, I was able to take a leading role with the sheep during the lambing season.

If a sheep had not lambed in the three to four hours I had observed her isolating herself from the flock, I would coax her into the corner of the field, to catch her, to determine what difficulties she was encountering. Sometimes if she was a little

85

nervous, or on the wild side and difficult to catch, I set up a temporary fence of netting wire running five to six foot away from the hedge and running in a slight vee formation a few yards long up to one corner of the orchard. By coaxing the sheep into this run of fencing you could guarantee catching her where the fence met the corner of the orchard. Clasping her with one hand round the neck, and with the other reaching under her udder, you caught the back leg farthest away from you, drawing it towards you to coax her to gently lay on her side. There were a variety of reasons why a sheep can run into difficulty with lambing, as with any type of animal with four legs. It can be a breach birth, meaning the lamb is about to be born backwards, feet first. In this situation when giving assistance you would act fast, to draw the lamb out to prevent it from suffocating. Sometimes the lamb was in the right position, but only one leg was in its correct position, under its chin, in the forward position, so you would have to push the lamb back temporarily to get your hand in to draw the other foot forward first, to allow a normal birth to happen, with some quick assistance, because by now the ewe would be in some state of exhaustion. She may have given birth to one but was showing signs that another was due, to find on inspection the second would have been a stillbirth. It was wise to deliver the dead lamb, for if you did not, it could result in loosing the ewe because of the ultimate decomposing that would be taking place in her womb. Once the lamb is delivered you would clasp your hand over the nose and round the upper part of the jaw, near the eyes and draw it down over the mouth to clear the airways of after birth, often referred to as 'the cleansing'. If it did not start breathing immediately, you would massage the lunges by a rotating movement against the chest cage with one of its front feet. This would normally last for only a few moments, so you would then place the lamb near the mouth of the exhausted sheep who would immediately start to lick the lamb with her sandpaper rough tongue, cleaning off all the mucus. This simple act of cleaning will stimulate the lambs circulation, and with the gentle murmurings from the ewe start to build a bond with the lamb. While the sheep is laying on her side, it was wise to turn her up onto her rump between your thighs and check that the udder was in good order, with both sides producing good milk, and no sign of mastitis. Mastitis will be evident, if on the first draw, they're were clots in the milk, and will need an antiseptic injected into the udder. If there were any permanent damage to either side of the udder, you would not keep her for another season. You now gave needed time for the sheep to clean the lamb and for them to find their feet, and the lamb to get its first feed. At birth the udder has a copious amount of cholesterol, which sits at the base of the udder, which will be drawn off when the lamb first sucks, with the prime purpose of stimulating the heart and circulation, in the first vital moments the lamb has been born. Sometimes it was wise to turn the ewe onto her rump and ensure the lamb did get the first feed easily. I would carry a small bottle of cholesterol in my pocket, for if there were twin lambs born, you would catch the second lamb born, pour a little of the cholesterol into the cap, then dip my finger in and get the lamb to lick it off, just in case the first lamb had drawn off all the cholesterol from both sides of the udder.

After the new born lambs and their mother had got their strength back, while I went on walk about to check what was going on with the rest of the flock, I would then return to take them back to the farm paddock close to the farmstead. Foxes will feed on the after birth, and attack the weak newborn lambs, so by bringing them close to home you could keep a wary eye on them and give the sheep a change in diet to help with their milk production. Trying to drive the sheep and her lambs will always end up in failure. Because of the maternal instincts of the ewe she will be spending her time turning round and running back to the lambs murmuring reassurances instead of moving on with them following. So you would catch the lamb or lambs by the front feet, and pick them up with their rear feet and body hanging in a relaxed way, just in the same position they were in the womb. You then went ahead with the ewe dutifully following. If it was the ewes first season for giving birth, you needed to be patient, for the ewe would occasionally abandon the lambs as you carried them in front. After putting the lamb down a few times, standing back and allowing the sheep to return, she would soon get the message and stay with you and keep following.

One early morning I had brought a ewe home with her lamb, temporarily leaving her in the rickyard while I went in for breakfast. When I came out from the farmhouse to take them to the paddock, I found a second dead lamb close by. While I had been at breakfast, unknowing she was about to have a second

87

lamb, but mainly due to exhaustion from bearing the first and bringing her back to the farm, she had not got up immediately the lamb was born, and had allowed the lamb to suffocate on the after birth. I was quite upset, yet annoyed at not being there when it was born, to prevent this loss.

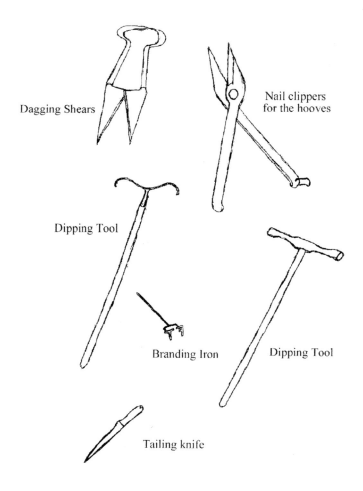

Plate 6:2 The Shepherds tools.

Right through the season shepherding is very labour intensive, but is very rewarding work, especially in spring at lambing time.

A period of wet weather can be quite devastating during the lambing season. A freshly born lamb born in the cold wet rain can soon die of hypothermia if its fleece gets saturated with cold rain. Sheep farmers welcome a cold frosty spell during the lambing season with a daily spattering of sunshine. Once the ewe has cleaned the new born lamb it will stay dry, with the thick fleecy curls keeping it warm, and much to your delight you will soon see them in small groups scampering and dancing on any tree stump or embankment oblivious to danger while the mothers quietly graze.

After lambing was over we continued to feed the sheep with concentrates and oatmeal, now introducing mangolds into the diet. Our neighbour often fed his ewes mangolds before they lambed, resulting in a number of prolapses. If a sheep died leaving an orphaned lamb, or a ewe had triplets, you would hand rear them, taking the weaker one from the ewe with triplets. If a lamb was weak, small or looking sickly you would bring it home, with its mother, then put it in a fruit box with a bed of straw, often in the farm house kitchen, with an infrared lamp hanging overhead, to give warmth, and regularly feed it with milk and glucose. If a ewe lost her only lamb, then you would take one of the suckling lamb referred to as a tiddler, and get the ewe to adopt it. You would first catch the sheep and put her into an enclosure. This can be a makeshift pen made out of a few bales stacked two high, with a hurdle as a gate. Then you would skin the dead lamb, put a slit in the two rear legs of skin and poke the rear legs of the live lamb through, draping the rest of the skin over the back of the lamb for adoption, tying the skin of the front legs round its neck. It may mean you will have to hold the ewe a few times while it feeds, for if she is wary of it, sometimes she will fight the lamb off, so you would have to keep them separate, except for feeding. After two or three days she will normally take to it, and both be able to join with the other lambs and ewes.

When the first batch of lambs are turned three weeks old you would bring them into the farmstead, to have their tails cut and the ram lambs castrated. I thought I would ignore the advice of Dad and the rule of shepherding when lambing and take the sheep dog with me to round them up and drive them through the first gateway into the meadow next to the farmyard. As normal on entering the paddock I ordered the dog to round up the flock.

Instead of the sheep immediately running the opposite direction away from the dog, the sheep on seeing him approaching, instinctively ignored him and ran straight to their lambs to defend and protect them. Then when the dog started to close in towards the ewes with the lambs, the ewes swiftly turned round and went straight for the dog, head down endeavouring to butt him and get him air-born. The sheep as well as the lambs were oblivious to the danger of the dog, although frightened and confused. With all the noise and mayhem from the sheep, the dog was not able to hear me and was unsure what he was supposed to do. Having very quickly learnt my lesson, returned home with the dog, tied him up, rustled up as many helpers as I could, and returned to the paddock to quietly but firmly drive the sheep up to the gateway and through into the driveway. It meant a great deal of patience, for at times I had to carry the lambs forward to get one ewe to move forward, in order to get the flock to pursue. Once in the pen each of the older lambs were caught, and with a razor sharp knife the tail was quickly severed between a joint about two inches from the rump. The purpose was partly to keep the tail area clean, preventing flies alighting and maggots developing, and for cosmetic reasons making them look good, when market time came. At the same time they were castrated using the bloodless method, and given an injection in the front thigh against pulpy kidney, so that the lump formed by the injection would not catch the clippers at shearing time. The slightly distraught lamb once transferred into the next pen would race off to its mother, rushing to have a feed of milk to bring some comfort, unaware of the short stub of the tail vigorously wagging as it sprayed blood everywhere. In minutes the tail would stop bleeding. After all the lambs had gone through you would be eager to count the tails, just to know how many lambs we had, and to see what percentage per head of sheep that your flock was producing, because counting the lambs while in the field was nigh impossible. On tidying up the tails were thrown into a sack and placed by the garden fence. They made excellent manure base to go in the trench of the runner bean row. When the lambs had reached the fourteen weeks old, they were separated from the ewes for weaning. You would find it disturbing for a night or two because they would be baa-ing and bleating, calling to one another all day and night till they had settle down.

90

Come early June and the shearing of their fleeces would commence. The sheep would again be brought down from the field into the catching pens. At the end of the set of pens a large tarpaulin was laid out as a working platform, giving sufficient area to shear the sheep and to roll the fleeces up, to prevent dirt and grass picking up in the fleeces. Along one side of the tarpaulin a stake was driven into the ground and the shearing machine set up and attached to keep it rigid. The sheering machine once had a handle to be turned by hand in former days, but now a belt pulley had replaced the handle. Dad's ingenuity came into play, for the two-wheeled tractor, the Autoculto, which had been used for moulding the potatoes, was now to be used to drive the shearing machine. The Autoculto was placed onto a pair of fruit boxes, which lifted the wheels off the ground. The pulley belt was attached to the shearing machine, and then placed round the one wheel. The Autoculto was started and the wheels started, to ensure the one wheel is in line, and to tension the belt. Then two pairs of stakes would be driven into the ground, one set in the front and one set at the rear of the Autoculto framework to keep the Autoculto firmly fixed. Dad would have a helper to catch the sheep, and while he was shearing the helper would be rolling up the fleece from the previous sheep that had been shorn. Having caught the sheep you led her onto the tarpaulin, and by leaning over her front shoulders holding her neck with your left hand and taking the front right leg with your right hand pick her front up, which will cause her to lose her rear footing, ending on her rump. Alternately you could bring your right hand under her udder and catch her back left leg, drawing it up under her stomach, which would have the same effect. You then ensured she was comfortable, with her rump on the ground, and her back nestled between the inners of your legs. The one catching the sheep would be close by to aid dad when shearing by first handing the clippers. The pride of the shearer is to cut the fleece off in one piece and the sheep looks tidy once shorn. There is always the danger of cutting a fold of skin with the clippers, so a container of antiseptic powder was always at hand to dry up the wound, to prevent the inevitable attack of flies which will lay eggs, and in turn infest the sheep with maggots in a matter of hours.

Holding the sheep's head by taking her jaw in your left hand or her neck and head under the left elbow and arm, you would start by running the clippers a few times down the centre of the stomach to the udder, drawing the fleece open to either side, each time you made a pass. Once you reached the edge of the thighs, and trimmed down, away over the rear legs, you would work round each side of the stomach stopping close to the centre of her back by gently leaner her sideways.

Placing your right foot between her rear legs and gently leaning the head to one side over your thigh you drew the clippers upwards along the underneath of the neck, transferring the sheep's head to the other thigh, working along either side till the whole of the neck was shorn. By now the sheep would be sitting slightly sideways, with only the back to be shorn. So keeping the left hand firmly around the neck you gently lowered the sheep down between your legs shearing down the back towards the tail with her being slowly drawn onto her side. Then if it was a large sheep which was just too long to reach the tail you would immediately draw your leg nearest the head across the neck which by now was on the floor, using the leg and foot as a noose, with you ending up on your knees, to finally trim the base of her back and tail. As soon as you stood up, by a gentle nudge of her rump she was up and away. A good sheerer in competition will shear a sheep in 3 minutes, but working continuously a good shearer could on average shear a sheep every 5 minutes.

So once Dad had received the next sheep for shearing, John or Jack whoever was helping him at the time would prepare the fleece for folding. The fleece would be dropped onto the tarpaulin with the outer side facing up and neatly spread out. Taking a pair of dagging shears, they would remove any lumps of muck from the tail end, and any bits that were knotted by dirt, throwing them into a bucket, to await the bean row. Each of the leg sections were thrown over into the centre back portion of the fleece and the sides folded in until the width of the fleece was about 18" wide. Kneeling down at the tail end, they would start to roll the fleece tightly and firmly up to where the neck commenced. Placing one knee on the fleece to prevent it unfolding, they then took the neck portion, twisting it into a rope, and stretching it sufficiently long enough to rap once around the rolled up fleece and then tuck it under itself. The fleece was then placed in a very large woolsack. The rams were always left till last purposely because they took longer to be shorn, and could be more difficult to handle, because of their size. Shearing is a very backbreaking job, yet the oils of the fleeces are very good for the hands, and is used in the making of some types of soap.

Plate 6:3   Hubert Yates

It was at that time legal requirement that the flock are dipped to prevent pests attacking them, such as the blowfly that lay their eggs and hatch into maggots. If the sheep is left undetected the maggots will eat deep into the flesh, with the sheep eventually dying. Alongside the dipping bath was an 18-inch wide tray for the sheep to walk through to reduce foot rot. In a damp summer or where foot rot was predominant the sheep would be frequently taken through the trough. The trough was just in the entrance to the rickyard. The drive and the surrounding area just inside the rick yard had to be cordoned off with sheep feeding racks to create a makeshift collecting pen.

Dipping begins with one farm hand catching the sheep and gently letting it down backwards into the tank. If you had more than three sheep in the tank at any one time, you would not be able to control them or prevent one of them escaping up the steps at the other end while trying to dip the others. For some years it was a legal requirement for the local policeman to call to ensure that you were dipping all your sheep and you did the job properly. Before the introduction of plastic aprons, rubber leggings and wellingtons, each person helping would wear a leather apron to protect them from getting thoroughly wet. The sheep would automatically want to swim to the exit side of the tank, so Dad with a specially made dipping tool, a wooden handle with a tee shaped attachment, would gently and continuously turn their heads as they sought to swim to the exit. As he drew them back and round a couple of times he would draw the tool from under the neck and place it on the top of the front shoulders and press them down briefly to allow the head to be submerged into the dip. The sheep weighed down by the liquid would emerge from the tank with the dip gushing from the fleece onto the concrete floor of the small pen at the exit, and drain back into the tank. When the pen was full you needed to judge the right time to release the sheep, because moments after the sheep had emerged, and most of the weighty liquid had drained, the sheep would give an almighty shake of her body showering everything within a four to five feet radius.

Despite passing the sheep through the footbath and the dipping tank they could still get foot rot or maggots, so you could not take the chance of missing your daily look at the flock. It only took a couple of days for maggots to eat deep into the sheep's flesh, letting infection get in. You would scrape off the maggots, soaking the area with disinfectant and may be give an antibiotic injection.

In mid-summer you would need to bring the lambs back to the farm at least twice for drenching, that is, give them a medicine through the mouth to treat them for worms. Again the lambs would be driven into the catching pens to make it easy for catching and monitoring that they had been drenched. The drench solution has to be diluted before being administered. One season, after Dad had drenched a dozen or so lambs, he noticed some with their heads hanging low, starting to pant and have difficulty breathing. They then began to slump down onto their side very bloated, to find one or two already dead. On checking the instructions on the bottle he discovered to his horror that he had not mixed the solution to the recommended dilution. He immediately ran and telephoned the vet to be told there was nothing he could do about it, and consequently all those already drenched soon died. After viewing the scene, I made myself scarce, hearing John quote Dad's famous quote "*That **blessed** kid*", which I often had quoted about me when Dad was feeling irate and looking for someone to blame. I knew that somewhere along the line of events I was likely to get the blame, although I cannot recall doing anything to cause this tragedy to happen on this occasion.

Towards the end of the summer and into the mid-autumn, every few weeks or so as the lambs matured they would be graded from the flock and sent to market. Any broken mouthed ewes, that is ewes whose teeth were starting to deteriorate, and had bred four or five seasons, or ewes that were barren, would all be culled out and sold. If a sheep sale turned out to be a wet day, it could be an advantage, for as the farmers could not do much work back at home more would attend, with the chance of the lambs making a good price. While at the sale Dad would be on the look out for some teg lambs to buy, those of two years old, to take back home to keep the size of the flock up, and maybe buy a young ram to bring in some fresh blood.

Two of the shepherds unwanted pastimes, was looking for sheep that had got out, and repairing the broken fences. There is always one in the flock who seems to think that the grass on the other side of the fence is better. The sheep that is regularly trying to get out often stands out from the rest of the flock by having little wool round her neck, from pushing through gaps in the hedgerows. If one sheep finds a gap invariably others will follow. Normally it is relatively easy to find them, for they will be wandering up and down the hedge row trying to find their way back or you will see the traces of wool where they have got out, and their feet would have left trace marks in the soil, and on the road they would have left their droppings and lumps of mud from between their claws. The difficult job was often getting them back, especially if they had wandered far, sometimes having to go back to the farm to get extra help to stand in farm driveways and road junctions to direct them back into the field. If you had espied them soon enough, and they were only a short way away from where they got out, a quick shout, or a quick chase from behind them by the dog, would let them know of your disapproval and they would often automatically run back and through the gap they had got out through. Once the sheep were back in the field, you would hastily get some hedge trimmings, if available, or go into the coppice and get some nice long pieces of hazel branches and weave them into the butt of the hedge to fill the gap or glat as it was often termed.

Having regularly attended Sunday school and chapel my family and our Christian friends had shown me that we were *all like sheep having gone astray, we are really born as orphans, without a spiritual father.* Through watching the behaviour of the sheep I realised that we all have the option to return to God's fold under the care of Jesus the Good Shepherd. At the age of eleven it was very simple for me to ask the Good Shepherd in prayer to come and take care of me and guide me through the rest of my life. I had to admit to Him that I had been a wanderer all those years, and needed Him to forgive me for all my misdeeds. After all, He had laid down His own life for His sheep. So just by taking that initial approach to Him, and because He is never changing, though I have got into some terrible scrapes at times, my life is so fulfilled and satisfied, knowing that He always, has supreme control of my life, and will not allow me to come to any terminal harm. The hymn writer has summed it up beautifully as he relates the love of the Good Shepherd from Psalm 23.

THE KING OF LOVE my Shepherd is,
Whose goodness faileth never;
I nothing lack if I am His
And He is mine forever.

Where streams of living water flow
My ransomed soul He leadeth,

And where the verdant pastures grow
With food celestial feedeth.

Perverse and foolish oft I strayed,
But yet in love He sought me,
And on His shoulder gently laid,
And home rejoicing brought me.

Chapter 7

The Dairy Herd

With the ever-rising wages to farm labourers, and the increase in mechanisation, Dad sought alternate ways of farming to reduce the manpower. Although milking twice a day meant you were tied to the cowshed seven days a week, you could guarantee a monthly income from the Milk Marketing Board. He reduced the labour force to one dairy assistant, by cutting out growing roots and corn, selling the flock of sheep, and concentrating only on producing milk.

Once the decision to go into dairying was confirmed, some structural changes had to be made to the cowshed. A small lean to building was needed to accommodate the dairy, where all the milk would be cooled and put into churns. With chisels and sledgehammers, the entire floor of the cowshed was gutted. Hygiene was of utmost importance, with all the walls having to be plastered over to make it easy for washing down. To help some of the costs, dad swept the ceilings clean of cobwebs and attached strips of hard board, to prevent grain and dust creeping through the floorboard from the granary upstairs. A wall of concrete blocks, created a passageway three feet wide along the back of the cowshed behind the manger. The passageway was to enable him to feed the cows, and give room to house a few bags of feed. 18-inch diameter terracotta drainpipes were split along their length, with the halves used to create the manger. There was an art to splitting the drainpipes. The builders carefully packed the pipe with sand, and then skilfully chiselled a fine line down each side until the two halves split apart. Galvanised tubular dividers were fixed at right angles to the passage back wall and floor standing area, to allow a cow to be chained either side, but room enough for you to work in between while milking took place. An added luxury, attached to the dividing rail above the manger was an automatic water bowl. Up until now any animals kept indoors, had to have their water carried to them in buckets, but each of these bowls, which were just big enough for the cow to put her nose into, had a small flat plate inside at the rear, which when pressed, opened a valve to allow a measured amount of water through. On the floor immediately behind where the cows stood was a three-feet wide gully, four inches deep, to take all the muck and waste. The diary where all the milk was cooled stood on the left hand side at the entrance to the cowshed. At the other end, outside the cowshed, was a small lean-to building to house the vacuum machine that worked the milking plant. It had an electric motor for normal use, but positioned adjacent was a petrol motor. When there was an electrical power cut, which normally happened during thunderstorms, the drive belt was swopped over, and the petrol engine started. Suspended over the cow's heads, and into the dairy, running from the vacuum pump house, through the cowshed, was a stainless steel tube with a tap at each cow standing, where a rubber pipe would be attached from the milking buckets. Outside on the right-hand side running alongside the cowshed entrance, was the main bottom cattle yard, which had recently been covered in, with a collection pen positioned opposite the dairy. Around the two outer sides of the main yard was a manger and above a hayrack, which could be accessed from the outside, when feeding. The main yard had been open to the sky, but along the rear were a length of wooden shelters opening into the yard, with tiled roofs, which all had to be taken down. During the demolition I was permitted to drive the Field Marshal around the yard to assist in pulling down some of the large posts, and to back the trailer in to carry the rubble away. One day while innocently driving the Field Marshal across the cattle yard there was a sudden bang, with water gushing up the side of the mudguard from one of the rear tyres, spraying everywhere with some force. I had not noticed that close to where one of the posts to the building had been was the jagged end of a cast iron water down-pipe sticking out of the cobbled yard, which I had run straight over. Although Dad was displeased, much to my surprised he immediately rang J. C. Baker's tyre service to come out and repair the tyre without me getting into any serious bother.

On a lighter note, during the time Dad had been painting the new gate that led out of the collection yard into the cowshed, he had left the tin of paint on the floor near to the dairy with the stirring stick across the top. While I was standing by busily admiring his work, I felt the bolt upright tail of one of the young cats brushing against my leg. She then innocently walked past the wet paint stick on top of the tin, which attached itself to her tail. As she moved forwards she immediately became aware of the stick dragging behind her as the other end fell off the tin and onto the ground. Soon as she heard the stick noisily dragging on the ground behind her she leaped forwards onto the gate of the newly erected yard, shot up and clutched onto the top rail of the hayrack, racing along at great speed trying to escape the intruding item. As she darted along the rail, the bottom end of the sagging end of the stick repeatedly whacked each rail, creating a melodious rhythm like a xylophone, echoing up into the hollow roof of the building, causing the frightened cat to frantically leap forward at increasing speed until the stick finally fell off, she then jumped onto the rear wall at the other end of the yard.

After months of preparation, it was time to start to build the dairy herd, so Dad began by visiting one or two well established accredited herds of Ayrshires, those that were pedigree registered. These sales were for the purpose of selling off old stock, and surplus young in-calf heifers that were about to calve, and ready to start milking for the first time. He purchased about half a dozen older cows to start, that had a good record for large lactations, that is, high milk production. You would not normally keep cows for more than eight years for milking, although these cows had because of age, become more docile, and used to the milking machine. By having calves by A.I (artificial insemination) by a commendable accredited Ayrshire bull, they would produce a future generation of good milking cows. Each cow had a name, of which the oldest one was Doves Favourite. She was so docile, that if you sat a child on her back, she would continue to stand eating her cud. In the early part of her lactation, soon after the calf was born, her milk production built up to five gallons at each milking. For the first few weeks after calving, each day when milking time became imminent, the udder would grow immensely, so much so that when strutting through rutted gateways, while making her way to the cowshed, her teats would drag the ground, often with the milk gushing from the teats. Because she was producing so much milk you would have to keep a wary eye on the milking machine at this particular time, for as the milk bucket could only hold four gallons, and overflow into the vacuum tube overhead, fortunately ending up in a bucket attached to the vacuum line next to the pump, placed there for that very purpose. Doves Favourite was very much the build of an Ayrshire, being very slim. Willameno, one other of the cows purchased was unusually heavy built like the size of a bull, but still very docile. As the Ayrshire dairy cows are very slim, calving difficulties were few, so the calves produced were also very slim so if it were a bull calf, it would be no use to rear for beef and make little money when sold. It always pleased Dad when the cows produced a heifer calf, for it was the continuance of the herd.

Plate 7:1   Ayrshire cow with triplets

Calling the vet out at any time of day or night was daunting, but Dad had the ability to aid a cow when calving if it was large or breached. To assist the cow in calving he would tie each end of a six feet piece of rope to the protruding pair of calves legs, then looping the rope round his back to give added leverage pull the calf out. Sometimes, if it was a large calf, with the aid of a helper, he would put the rope round the calves head, and both persons would pull together holding onto a short pieces of broom handle attached to each end of the rope to get a firm grip.

Meanwhile John and May, together with their two children Simon and Judy had moved to a rented small holding in the village, and Willy Price had also found work in the village he came from, Dad's home village of Hoarwithy. This left the pair of semi-detached bungalows vacant. Needing further to reduce his work force Dad reluctantly had to make Jack Burraston redundant.

Fortunately Dad was able to get him fresh employment on the adjacent farm of Huntlands, run by Jack Payne. Dad immediately advertised for someone qualified in dairying, to live in the one bungalow, taking on Archie James and his family, from Bishops Frome.

Although I was not old enough to leave school I was cajoled into helping out with the milking, particularly at weekends.

At Whitbourne Primary School, once children had attained eleven years of age, and not succeeded in getting the eleven plus exam for the Grammar School they were sent to a finishing school at Brockhampton, near Bromyard. You had no opportunity to gain any qualifications at this school, so mum together with some of the mothers with children of my own age, were able to persuade the authorities to send us to the Secondary School over the border from Herefordshire into a Secondary Modern School in the city of Worcester.

Journeying to school involved getting up at 7.45am each morning, at the very latest. I would rush my breakfast down grab my satchel, I then launched myself onto my bicycle, ripping down the path behind the farmhouse onto the Gaines' back driveway that led to the main road. As it was a private drive I did not need lights in winter time, so it was quite hazardous, not quite knowing when the gates would suddenly appear, having to break rapidly. I would, swing the locked rear wheel round quickly to open the gate, then rush through, hoping it would shut without being told. After another high speed race, as I neared the main road gateway at the end of the drive, with both hands I gently pulled on the brakes, with one leg starting to dismount the bicycle, I would start to veer up over the embankment into the orchard aiming straight for the hedge. By now both feet would be firmly on the ground, and as I threw the bicycle into the side of the hedge, after a couple of long strides, would leapfrog over the gate, dashing across the main road hoping the bus had not beaten me.

Every fortnight Archie, the milking assistant, would have a weekend off and take his two weeks statutory holiday leave during the summer. So come hail or sunshine, whether it was school term or holidays, I had to take Archie's place. I was only thirteen when I was accosted into helping, so at 6.00am Dad would come into the bedroom without invitation and roll all the sheets and covers from me onto the foot of the bed, in distinctive tone "*Come on*

102

*David, **shift yourself***". " As soon as I heard him start to trot back down the stairs I would immediately drag the clothes back over me and snuggle under the eider down, but not for long. He knew my routine and just before going out to the dairy would give another shout.

As the house was over five hundred years old, one of our windowsills in the bedroom had rotted leaving a half-inch gap underneath. There was no heating and the gap produced a very icy draught in mid-winter. On cold winter nights, Mum would put a hot water bottle in the bed. At night when I went into the bedroom I would first get the clean shirt for morning, that's if I was going to school and not working on the farm, and roll back the eider down. In strict order, I would start to undress from the waist down, laying the clothes on top of the blanket in line with where my body would be and then leap into bed. My pullover, shirt and vest would swiftly leave my back, to land on top of my trousers, etc. Afterwards I would slide swiftly under the sheets pulling the eiderdown over my body, sometimes right over my head, if it was a desperately cold night. Next morning I would have a ready warmed set of clothes to put on, before leaping down the stairs, two steps at a time, to finish dressing by the warm log fire that Dad would have just re-kindled.

The mornings that I was having to help in the dairy, Dad had to return from the cowshed to the house, dismantling his wellingtons at least twice at the front door, before I would eventually get up. Dad would have been out in the dairy for at least half an hour before I joined him, preparing the equipment for milking the cows and putting feed into the mangers for the first lot of milking cows.

Dad, before getting up would spend a short time in prayer to ask God for direction, and help for the day, routinely getting up at 5.15am. Once down stairs and while the rekindled fire was coming to life, he spent a few minutes to read a passage from the bible, to keep his soul in good trim. He would then make both of us a cup of tea, leaving me a portion of bread and butter to eat which gave me time to come to. I loved to dunk the bread and butter in the tea, partly because I was too tired to eat it. In winter before going outside I would often add another pullover before putting my boiler suit on, which kept you snug and warm round the waist.

Slipping a pair of fisherman's socks over my ordinary socks, with cap jacket and gloves, I made my way to the back door.

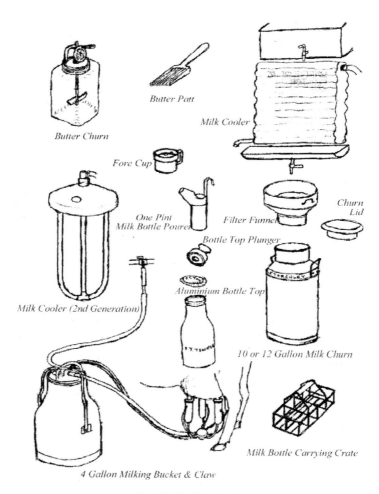

Butter Patt

Milk Cooler

Butter Churn

Fore Cup

One Pint Milk Bottle Pourer

Filter Funnel

Churn Lid

Bottle Top Plunger

Milk Cooler (2nd Generation)

Aluminium Bottle Top

10 or 12 Gallon Milk Churn

Milk Bottle Carrying Crate

4 Gallon Milking Bucket & Claw

Plate 7:2 The Dairy Parlour.

Having slipped my wellingtons on in the outhouse, taking a sturdy stick in my hand which leaned against the entrance, I would set off up to the field to fetch the cows in. It was necessary to bring the cows in to be milked, in time for the milk lorry to collect the churns at 8-30am. Through the winter we were obliged to keep the cows in the cattle yards, but as autumn and early winter approached it was pitch black outside setting out at this time in the morning. After heavy rain, the areas around the gateways where the cows assembled, would get very muddy, with holes, up to twelve inches deep full of water where the cows had regularly placed there feet, dragging themselves, squelching noisily through the gateway. By detecting the reflection of the moon on the water, I would try to step on the firmer soil around the edge of the holes filled with water. But, because the soil was so slippery, one foot would occasionally slip into a hole with my toe twisting forward and straight down, my wellington getting firmly stuck in the mud. As I was trying to rectify my balance with the other foot, I automatically tried to lift the foot stuck in the muddy hole forward to place it onto the next firm place, but no; the wellington stayed firmly fixed. My foot slid out of the wellington and straight down another hole, spraying water up my leg, soaking my foot and both legs,. I dare not hesitate, but refit the wellington while standing on one foot, and press on with collecting the cows, with the urge to get back to the farm as quickly as possible. With one half of my mind set on getting the cows back to the farm the other half of me was hoping Dad was in a good frame of mind and allowed me get changed, for by now I may not be in his good books, for having wasted his time getting up, and having to wait for the cows to come in, to get started.

Because it was wintertime invariably there was little grass, and the cows would be hungry, so most if not all the cows would be waiting at the gate. As with most animals, there was a pecking order, with the same cows exiting the field first, starting to divert down the roadside to get a bite of fresh grass on the verge. You would have to slip through the herd and swiftly turn the wanderers back, and then return into the field and follow those that always lag behind.

Any heifers due to calve for the first time, will join the herd a week or two before calving, to accustom them to the routines of milking. Introducing them to the cowshed, the manger, and getting

105

used to being tied up, calls for a little patience, having to coax them a few times into the stalls with the help of some rich cow cake or nuts. Then with some one standing behind the heifer, you would gently lean over her neck, reaching for the chain and tie her up. While the heifer is settling down to the parlour, listening to the sucks and hisses of the milking machines working, it is good to gently apply some cream to the udder or bag, as it is commonly referred to, to keep it supple but also to get the heifer used to being handled.

Before the milking machine suction cups are connected to the udder, the udder is washed, and then a small amount of milk is drawn out of each quarter, that is each part of the udder to determine that there are no signs of mastitis. A specially designed cup is used to squirt the milk into, having a ridge or lip around the inner top of the cup, where a stiff rubber platform sits. Mastitis has large milky clots, which will have settled down, in the lower part of the inside of the udder. If there is mastitis evident, as soon as you start to draw off any milk, a copious amount of clots will be seen immediately, falling onto the rubber platform. To prevent the mastitis-infected quarter being milked with the rest, the teat cup will be tied up allowing the other three quarters of milk into the bucket. The quarter will be milked by hand, then with a throwaway plastics syringe dad would inject an antiseptic into the udder, through the teat. Afterwards, with two fingers firmly pressed round the end of the teat, with two other fingers positioned above, would gently slide the fingers up the outside of the teat, to force the antiseptic up into the main part of the udder quarter.

Archie, when washing the cows udder, had a habit of standing behind the cow, one hand grabbing the top of her tail on her back to keep his balance and leaning against the side of the rear leg, down to the side of the cow, to get to the teats. He wore a long brown cow gown, with deep pockets at chest and hip height on both sides, which quite often were not buttoned up. During April when the cows are let out into the meadows, the spring grass makes their stomachs very loose. When following the cows in for milking you have to keep your distance for fear of getting sprayed. One spring Archie was going through the normal way of washing the udder, leaning over from behind, when unbeknown to him the cow lifted her tail. On full power, like the jet of a hosepipe, she shot warm fresh manure straight across the cowshed alleyway, not before she had loaded Archie's lower pocket full, and sprayed the full length of the cow gown with the green hot liquid. We did not charge him for his free delivery of fresh manure, but his wife was not a little put out with having to wash the coat.

For the first two or three days after the cow gave birth, the milk when boiled, would curdle into clots, due to the high amount of cholesterol in the milk, making it unsuitable to mix with the rest of the saleable milk. A pint of milk from a freshly calved cow would be taken into the kitchen and boiled up to see if it curdled. As soon as it stopped curdling the milk could go for sale.

While the last amount of milk from the main herd is being cooled, it was time to milk the heifer. You always left a freshly calved heifer to last, because she would take longer to milk, requiring both herdsmen's help to settle her down and accept the milking machine. When attempting to put the first two cups of the machine onto the teats, the heifer would repeatedly lift her back foot, kicking into the base of the udder, in an attempt to pull the machine off. So Dad would attach a piece of rope to the base of the tail and pass the other end between the udder and around the front of the back leg, against the front of the knee joint. Then as Dad gently attached each teat cup to the teats, the assistant will hold the rope firmly. As the heifer tries to kick, the rope will pull on the tail, reducing her desire to kick out. When fitted to the udder, the milking teat cup set, which is referred to as a claw, has a knob on the underside where the cups join. Once the cow has finished being milked, the knob under the cluster is pressed, which will cut off the vacuum supply, and the cluster then can be easily removed. It has the added advantage that if a cow occasionally drags the claw off with her foot, it will automatically cut off the supply the moment the knob hits the concrete floor, preventing loss of vacuum to the other units, and prevent dirt being drawn up the tubes.

When milking a freshly calved heifer, I as the assistant always ended up holding the rope, but as the heifer began to settle down, and become part of the milking routine, Dad would leave me to hold the rope and ensure the heifer stayed still, while he tended the last of the cows being milked, or started to clear the cowshed of milking machines, ready to let the last of the herd back into the yard.

For a while after a cow calved you would leave the calf with the cow until it had had its first full feed, then immediately wean the calf away. If it were a bull calf it would be sent straight to market for veal. If it were a heifer calf, it would be kept on for breeding and milking. For the first three to four months it would be fed with dried milk, while making available a small quantity of slender juicy rich hay, and a supply of calf nuts. As soon as the calf was weaned from its mother it will need to learn to drink milk out of a bucket. You had to coax the calf, by allowing her to suck your finger, then draw her nose into the bucket, with much of the milk spilling onto the ground until she gets used to the idea.

Quite often after the cow has calved you discovered she has no strength in her legs and refused to get up. This was due to a high deficiency of magnesium, so you would always keep at close hand a couple of litre bottles of magnesium liquid, and feed it intravenously into a vain in the neck, holding the bottle up shoulder high until the bottle was empty. Within a couple of hours the cow would of her own accord be up and on her feet.

In the spring the fresh grass brings an increase to the milk yield and higher butterfat content, so we planned for the cows to calve just after Christmas, after their nine-month gestation. Within a few days of calving, we expected each cow to increase her output of milk, so by mid spring the entire herd would be in the peak of milk production.

The second advantage to calving the cows down in late winter, and into the early spring, is that by late June, beginning of July the yield of milk begins to significantly drop, with less time having to be spent in the milking parlour. By now the cows will be out in the fields feeding for themselves, so there will be no feeding required, apart from a minimal amount of concentrated food given during the milking time. This frees up your time to spend on haymaking and harvesting.

Getting back to the milking parlour, once the cow has been washed, and a squirt of milk taken from each quarter to see it is healthy, and free from Mastitis, you pulled the cut off knob out to switch the vacuum on, producing a loud hissing noise, and placed each teat cup onto the teats. Each teat cup has an outer stainless steel body with a rubber inside tubular membrane. A pair of rubber tubes lead from the cluster to the bucket, both being drawn on, by the vacuum pump. The one larger tube takes the milk away, but before joining the bucket, a short observation glass is integral to indicate when the cow has finished milking. Another smaller pair of tubes, moulded in tandem, are attached to the cluster, drawing the vacuum, splitting up between the two pairs of outer stainless teat cups. The smaller moulded tubes are attached to a pulsatator on the bucket, which controls the rate of vacuum, pulsating every two seconds, alternating between each pair of teat cups, shrink the inner teat cup tube, to draw the milk down the teat. Once the milking cluster is taken off the cow, the milking unit is carried to the walkway behind the cows and the milking cluster swapped onto another empty bucket, to be used on the next cow. The bucket of milk is taken to the dairy to be cooled. In the early days the milk would have been poured into a shoulder high tank, where the milk would flow through a tap and over the outside of a brass radiator, with cold water flowing through. At the base of the radiator was a wide gutter, which drew the milk together through another tap into the churn, through a funnel fitted with a muslin filter. Later a much neater cooler was developed comprising of a framework, with a propeller inside, joined at the base by three tubes coming out of the underside. The cooler unit sat on top of the churn, with the three tubes hanging down inside the churn of milk. A hose pipe was attached to the top of the cooler, so when the water was switched on, the water drove the propeller, rotating the cooler tubes, cooling the milk on the inside and then returned back up into the framework and through small holes over the outside of the churn, giving a second chance for the water to cool the milk from the outside.

Occasionally during the dark winter months, you would go out to the assembly yard to fetch the last group of cows in for milking to discover one was missing. Because it was so dark when you went to fetch the herd in, you could not count them, and could not see if any cows were away over at the far side of the field. While you were contemplating having to return to the field to search for her, you would hear from some distance up the farm driveway a cow giving out a distressing "*Moo!*" as if to say what rights have you to go without me. You could tell by the jerky sound in her voice that she was running. By the outside lights of the cowshed you would look out to see her aimlessly cantering down the yard, with her udder swinging to and fro side to side from in front of her back legs, slowing down a pace as she approached the cowshed.

In winter, when all the cows had been turned back into the yard, and while Dad is filling the card labels with his name and quantity of gallons tying them onto the churn handles, Archie will in his own words *"be ginning um cows sum aye"*.

I was told the tale about a farmer boasting to his neighbour about how he had managed to teach his cow to go without food. After a long explanation of how he had managed it, he mentioned that he only had one disappointment. *"What was that?"* His mate asked, *"She went and died on me."*

During the spring and summer months, every two to three days or so, Dad or myself would take a can of petrol, cross the lane into the pear tree orchard, and wind our way through the coppice up to the Snygmore reservoir. In the late spring and summer I would take a sickle with me to keep the coppice path clear of brambles or nettles. The man made reservoir had a dam wall made out of stone, wide enough to drive a tractor across. On the outer side of the wall, at the foot of the reservoir was a small-galvanised hut with a petrol driven water pump. You filled the fuel tank of the pump from the petrol can to the brim and started the engine, allowing it to run until the fuel run out. The water was pumped up into a reservoir on the high point of the Stoneyfoot Orchard, and then ran back by gravity to two tanks, which were housed in the hedgerows of the adjacent fields. Occasionally the reservoir over flowed, if you had not gauged when the reservoir had dropped to a sufficient level to warrant the full tank of petrol. I used to enjoy the walk up to the reservoir pump house.

Walking through the coppice, and along the edge of a small stream, on a regular basis I enjoyed seeing the spring flowers and plants breaking out, like wood anemones, primroses, king cups, and bluebells. As well as seeing the wonders of nature in spring it was also enjoyable hearing the morning chorus of bird song, and seeing nature change through the summer season.

Once the local folk knew we were selling milk, they began enquiring as to if we would supply bottled milk to them. Already each morning our workmen were collecting their pintas in their aluminium and enamelled metal billycans. We could get a lot more money for the milk in bottles than in the churns, so we set about getting the necessary bottles and equipment to distribute. This meant laying out cash for bottles, carrying crates, a large batch of aluminium bottle tops with our name and address etched in, a measuring jug to fill the bottles, and a tool to press the tops on. Each morning Mother would come into the dairy as soon as the first churn of milk was cooled to fill the bottles, and press the tops on, before preparing our breakfasts. Meanwhile Dad would connect the small animal trailer to the Standard Vanguard car, and back the trailer up to the door of the dairy, calling someone to help load the churns into the trailer, then take them up to the milk stand on the roadside at the farm drive entrance. Because the milk lorry was not permitted to travel up the lane to collect our churns, for the first few weeks, Dad had to drive down to the end of the lane adjoining the main road and wait for the milk lorry, to assist the driver loading the churns onto the lorry. He now needed a vehicle to deliver the bottled milk around the villages, so he purchased a Vauxhall Dormobile van. It was a good all round vehicle, because it was used for us as a growing family, useful to take extra children with us to Sunday school. Monday morning I would have the job of taking the rear seats out to make space in the rear to carry the churns to the stand, as well as being used as a delivery van, for the bottled milk. Before I left school, Dad and Mum, did the milk round together, extending into our own village of Whitbourne and houses on Bringsty Common adjoining, taking up most of each morning, seven days a week. Mum spent some time knocking on doors in the early days to drum up a few more customers. Unfortunately the milk round had its draw back by eating into Dad's working day.

Because our herd was accredited, each cow had to have her milk weighed once a week. A member of the Milk Marketing Board would turn up each month unexpectedly, to take a sample of milk for analysis, and to rate how much butterfat was in the milk, which determined how much we got paid for the milk. The MMB member would also monitor us recording and weighing the milk from each cow. Sometimes they would turn up a day or so just after we had weighed, which gave us no little pleasure in having to weigh the milk from each cow all over again, in the same week, and waylay the normal finish time of milking. Paul and I found this weighing routine fascinating, so much so that we would each get a piece of brown card from a cereal packet, draw a few grid lines down and across the cardboard and create a spreadsheet. We persuaded dad to cut a piece of hardboard out for a base, and with a large bulldog clip make up our own weigh sheet. So each weigh day, when off school, we would follow the milking and as the bucket of milk was hooked onto the scales, we would jot down our own records, then hang the charts on the cowshed wall joining the official chart, till the next week. The fascination of spreadsheets, and creating records grew on me, with analytic work and spread sheets becoming an important part of my future career.

One unwelcome job that had to be done every two years was bringing all the cows, heifers and calves down to the farmyard to have their test for TB (Tuberculosis). The last cows milked would have to stay tied up in the cowshed, while the rest of the cattle would be put through the cow 'crush'. The 'crush' was a small cubicle, just large enough for one animal, with a clamp at the one end to hold the cow or heifers head, with a bar or gate at the rear to prevent them reversing out. The vet would have to visit twice, once to inject them with a TB reactor, and then the following week to take a skin thickness reading, which took much longer. While the vet was taking the skin thickness, one cowhand was taking a look in the animal's ear for a tattooed number or an ear tag, shouting out the pedigree registration number to a third hand who would be busy writing the tag or tattoo number and the measured results.

As the herd grew and the heifers began to come in for breeding, it became more economical to purchase a young bull a month or so old, again by visiting one of the accredited dairy herd sales. Straight away, the young bull had a halter, made of rope worn head, to teach him to be led. John would take him for a short walk up and down the farm drive, until he started to get too strong. The vet then had to pierce a hole in his nose and fit a ring. All dairy bulls are ferociously dangerous especially when they were brought out to serve the cows, making it very necessary for everyones' safety.

The young bull soon became too strong to be housed in the wooden pen, so we had to build a purpose built pen for him. The building behind the workshop was chosen because it was brick built, and was just the size for the bulls sleeping quarters. With the one side opened up into the stable yard, an outer yard was constructed and the cow service cubicle similar to a crush was attached alongside.

A set of 9" x 6" posts standing 6 feet out of the ground, were placed about 2' 6 " apart along the three outer sides of the outer yards, with a set of 9" wide concrete blocks cemented in between to about 4 foot high. Finally through 1.1/2 in. holes already cast in the top of the concrete posts were two lengths of galvanised piping.

To my surprise, as young as I was at the time, the builder had ordered grey, soft marl stone sand for the mix of cement between the concrete blocks.

Once the cement and concrete floor in the structure had set, we transferred the bull to his new home, to enjoy a little bit more freedom. Yet the space was not what he would be used to, when in the wild, so he would spend his time rubbing his lowered head against the side of the walls or swinging his head round, with one of his horn stubs bashing against it. A day had hardly passed when, while he was busy rubbing his head, and at time thumping the wall, we noticed the top of the wall moving to and fro about a couple of inches each time he hit it. The inferior mortar against the posts, had cracked all along the edge of the blocks, from the floor up, so we had to coax the bull into the covered-in sleeping and feeding area with some food, and close the three way gate. You were able to open the gate again to give him access to his main exercise yard, and when a cow needed serving, you could draw the gate further open to give the bull access to the cow standing in the crush. By pulling the gate further it would give access into the stable yard. To fix the walls we purchased strips of 2 ins. wide metal and attached two lengths on both sides of the wall, using rawlbolts firmly bedded into the concrete posts, making a very secure pen.

Young heifers were ready to breed at only eighteen months. So every two to three years we would be purchasing another young bull, and occasionally a young heifer, to prevent interbreeding, and to improve the herd.

Although I spent a good part of my time at school, I was able to pick up the seasonal and daily routines of the farm. My day at the Worcester School finished at 4-30pm, and then I would wend my way down to the bus stop on the A44 road in the centre of St. Johns, next to the Church, to await the No.420 Midland Red bus. The bus would reach the end of the Gaines drive about 5-15pm. On some rare occasions the bus would turn up at the St. Johns bus stop full, but because the bus company had an obligation to get school children home, they would charter a special bus for us.

In the late spring and during the summer months, for a change from travelling on the bus, and if I were out of school on time, I would rush down to the main city train in Foregate Street, and catch the steam train, which on arrival would take me as far as the Suckley junction, on its way through to Bromyard, about 1.1/2 miles from home. It was only in my mid-adult years, that I discovered the train stopped in the Henwick station in St. Johns, just a five-minute walk from school, which would have saved a ¼ hour dash down into the town. The steam train set off much earlier than the bus, so I would arrive at Suckley much earlier, but would have to walk the 1.1/2 miles home. It was summer and the walk was very enjoyable, walking up the Suckley road, under the railway bridge, turning right through a field gateway, cutting through the Clayfoot farm, and back down the Linley Green lane, getting me home in about the same time as journeying on the bus. I was told some years later, that I could have turned the other way out from the railway station along the Suckley road, and turning left down one of the cart roads, could have reduced my journey time by half. It showed how lonely my life was, and how little time the family had to support and help me, during my years at school.

One sunny warm afternoon, as I walked along the lane, from the railway station, and crossed over the farm boundary, up over the hill alongside the Hollow Orchard, I could smell and see traces of fresh farmyard manure on the lane. It was the start of the Easter break, and I knew that the cows were still inside, in the yards, and it would be a week or two before the cows were left out in the meadows at night, before the yards would be cleaned out. As the farm came into view, I could hear and see tractors and trailers loaded with the manure travelling at high speed up the lane towards the Tolladine field. I then noticed a JCB digger working in the Paddock alongside the farm driveway, and could see others in dark clothes, to discover one was a policeman, wandering to and fro along the driveway. This was right out of character with the routines of the farm, so I guessed something serious was wrong. When I reached the farm, I was informed that one of the cows, shortly, after turning her out into the yard, started to bleed from the mouth and rear. In a very short space of time she was

114

dead. The vet, Mr. Francis Anthony, who had only just joined the Bromyard practice was immediately called out, and diagnosed her as having Anthrax. Anthrax is a highly contagious disease, and can also be caught by human beings. The onset of this diagnosis called for very stringent statuary emergency measures to be implemented immediately. While every effort was being made to ensure that the rest of the herd, or anyone does not come in contact with the dead cow, the rest of the herd were moved out of the yard. Meanwhile Dad with the vet went into the house to telephone the various services, and inform the Police and the Ministry of Agriculture, to supervise the sterilisation requirements. Watkins and Griffith came and helped clean out the manure from the yards. The coal merchant needed to deliver a good quantity of coal to ensure the fire was strong enough to incinerate and consume the carcase. Once the JCB had finished digging the hole in the Paddock, the cow was dragged onto a tired old wooden gate, which had seen better days, and towed by a rope, attached to a tractor, up the yard to the hole. She was drawn over the hole, and the fire was lit. As the fire met the rungs of the gate and they caught light, the cow would fall into the pit. Once the cow was completely burnt, and the fire was out then the hole was filled in. The immediate area around the hole was then fenced off, and isolated from animals for seven years. The same isolation measures also applied to the field where the manure was spread. Once the yard was cleaned out, the yard and the sheds where the cows had been, had to be washed down. Then with the aid of a hand pump, all the walls and the floors, had to be sprayed with disinfectant, under the watchful eyes of the man from the Ministry. The date of the incident stands out as it happened on the Easter Friday, which meant the work had to carry on through the holiday weekend, till it was complete.

With the exception of one acre of potatoes, we gave up growing any root crops, and the growing of grain. Because we grew no corn, it meant having to buy in straw, which was purchased while still standing in the field, from farms in the locality. Once the farmer had cut the corn we would take our New Holland 68 baler to the field. Hauling the bales home with tractor and trailer was a long-winded way of haulage, so we purchased a Vauxhall flat bed lorry detaching the cattle box, greatly reducing road-travelling time. In later years, to improve the time of baling we employed Watkins and Griffith with their big round baler, and the help of a local haulage contractor with articulated lorries to assist us with the carriage back to the farm. It meant having to buy an additional set of hydraulic straw handling equipment, which fitted onto the front tractor loader, like a spike, to pick up the very heavy round bales onto the trailers, and position them at the bay. During the time we did have corn, we had a regular visit of the Mill mix lorry, which would grind the oats, adding concentrates to it. The mill mix lorry would draw the corn out of a silo, sat behind the bottom barn, then blow the crushed corn mixed with protein additives straight into a circular bin that we had sighted outside the dairy. The bin had a feeding auger built underneath, which went directly into the cowshed to feed to the cows.

I grew up in the farmhouse right up until I was in my mid twenties When I finally left school, having spent only eighteen months working on the farm, with the intervention and influence of my senior metal work teacher I went into engineering.

We still needed someone to help feed the younger heifers in the fields and help with haymaking and harvesting. Stan Griffith one of the partners in the agricultural contracting business introduced his sister Marg and her husband Hubert to Dad, as addition farm workers. They were offered the job, and moved into the other bungalow, that had once been lived in by John and May Hindle.

Each weekend Archie had off, up to the time I left the farm to work in engineering, I helped with the milking. When the autumn and winter cold started to set in, due to constantly dipping my hands in and out of the wash bucket, while washing the cow's udders, Eczema would break out where the arm and wrist reached into the water, and down over my knuckles. At times the topside of each finger would suddenly split open exposing the flesh, making them very painful. The wrists would also break out in an itchy rash. I tried to wear rubber gloves with gauntlets, but even with Talcum powder inside, my hands and wrists continued to sweat and go sore. Although I enjoyed working with the sheep, haymaking and harvest, milking cows was not for me. By the time I left the farm, Paul had left school and taken over. Soon after, Archie retired making the bungalow vacant. When my brother Godfrey left school, he joined the farm also, so Paul and Godfrey both went to live in the bungalow. Then some years later, falling on hard times, Dad sold the bungalow that Paul and Godfrey were living in, to me, where we spent a further ten years together. During the mid 1980's the Milk Marketing Board, forewarned all the dairy farmers that they were going to cease using milk churns and start to send milk tankers around the farms to collect the milk. This meant another change to the farms milking systems. It meant that we would have a large stainless tank put into the dairy, having a double skin, filled with a coolant-circulating round. An extra stainless steel tube would have to run across the ceiling of the cowshed to carry the milk direct from the cows to the tank. In turn the Vacuum pump would have to be fixed at the other end of the cowshed, behind the dairy to draw the milk in the right direction into the tank. The milk buckets would no longer be required, with a new set of hoses fitted to suit the new flow system. The present floor arrangement in the cowshed, which at present meant a lot of back bending, was heightened where the cows stood, to make life easier. A new method of feeding the concentrates to the cows in the cowshed had been introduced. The feeding tube that came from the galvanised silo from outside the dairy, previously filled with meal, was now filled with cow nuts. A screw shaped auger inside the feeding tube was placed along the floor above the cowshed ceiling in the granary, to draw the nuts along, with outlets leading down into individual bins, over each pair of cows. With a ladle used for measuring, dad would transfer the correct amount from the bin into a smaller bin below, in readiness for the next cow to be milked. Then by pulling a leaver, it transferred into the manger. Once a day the auger was switched on, and would feed the bins, through the down pipes. Once each bin was full, the food would back up into the auger, continuing to the next bin, until it pushed the food against a pressure switch at the far end, and cut the auger off. While the changes were being made, Dairy Supplies of Hereford supplied a portable milking parlour, which sat outside the dairy in the main farmyard. For the first week it took a lot of patience and coaxing to get the cows into the portable parlour partly due to the similarity it had to a cow crush, anticipating a vet may be hovering around. The entrance to the parlour had been sealed off by gates and the farm lorry, The first afternoon milking took till 12-00pm at night, to get them all milked, with one cow trying to leap over the bed of the lorry to escape. When the work was finished it did take a little persuasion, and a little patience to get the cows up the new standing area, which was now about 12 ins. high.

GENUINE DISPERSAL SALE

of the entire
NMR RECORDED

DAIRY HERD

(79 HEAD)
of

HOLSTEIN - FRIESIAN CATTLE

for

F.J.TOWNSEND & SONS
OLD GAINES FARM, WHITBOURNE, WORCESTER.

removed for the convenience of sale to

THE CATTLE MARKET
WORCESTER

SATURDAY 30th MARCH 1996
11.30am.

AUCTIONEERS

McCartneys

THE CATTLE MARKET, WORCESTER, WR1 3NT.
TEL: 01905 612968 or 01584 872251

Plate 7:3 Dispersal sale catalogue

On approaching the door of the cowshed you would hear the occasional thud, to see one of the cows swinging her head against the smaller feed bins. Once the cows had finished their ration of food, they discovered that if they gave the bin a good clout with the top of their head, they could get some of the food to seep through the side of the smaller bin, and get an extra morsel from the ration that had been put ready for the next cow. Once each cow had been milked, by lifting a lever behind the cow, a gate would open in front of the cow, allowing her to walk out through the back passage and back into a second collection yard at the rear of the cowshed. The second collection yard was laid out in such a way, so as to enable you to drive a tractor in the centre gangway, with a large bale of hay or silage on the front forklift for feeding. When the milk tanker arrived, the driver would screw a hosepipe leading from the lorry onto the base of the tank in the dairy. Then he would take a reading from the long steel measuring rod inside the tank, before raising a lever handle with a sluice plate on the bottom, just inside the tank, leaving the tanker pump to do the rest. Every week or so, while the milk was being pumped out, the driver would take a small container of milk back with him to the laboratory for testing. It was not unknown for farmers to add a few gallons of water into the milk to bring in a little more money, until they got caught.

In the severe winter of 1986, due to heavy snowfalls and deep frosts, the milk tanker was unable to reach the farm for some days. The fuel in the tractors would get frozen, with Tilley lamps being kept alight in the dairy overnight to keep the water and the milk from getting frozen up. The loss of a collection meant there was nowhere to store the surplus milk from the next day's milking. For emergency measures, we had a collapsible tank to transport the milk, made out of polythene, which would sit on the bed of a trailer. During the first days of the freeze-up Dad discovered that the tanker was able to get as far as the local town of Bromyard, so he filled the tank and took the milk to meet it. The conditions were so bad that by the time the tractor had got to Bromyard the milk had started to freeze. So for the next few days, the edge of the trailer was padded with straw bales to protect the milk.

At the start of the 1990's it was becoming clear that the farm would not be able to continue to support all the partners that owned the farm. At this time, their were Dad, Mum, Paul and Godfrey who were the partners in the farm, with Paul and Godfrey both having growing family's to support. Much of the tractor work

119

was being carried out by the sub-contractors, cutting silage, hauling it in and placing it in the clamp, as well as carrying out the manure and spreading it, which put an enormous burden on the bank balance.

Initially by asking me to buy the bungalow that Paul and Godfrey were living in, went some way to help with the cash flow. Sadly, shortly afterwards, due to the cash crisis Dad had to make Hubert redundant. Thankfully due to contacts at work, I managed through a former colleague of mine, to get Hubert a job in Worcester. Then Paul decided to get married, so Dad had the unenviable task of asking Hubert and Marg to vacate the bungalow for Paul to live in.

The cash crisis continued to get worse, with the family having to sadly sell the farmhouse, and convert the top barn for Dad and Mum to live in. Meanwhile the two parts of the Bringsty field, as well as the Ham meadow, and the Gaines' orchard were sold off. Soon Godfrey got married, so the stables were converted for him and his wife Deb's to live in.

Dad and Godfrey were sharing the full responsibility of running the dairy herd, so with difficult negotiation, Paul's part of the partnership was bought out. This was a very distressing time for all the family.

For the next five years the routines of the farm began to settle down, until Mum's health began to fail, with Dad having to spend more and more time in the house, fearing Mum would wander off or do anything that would cause her injury. To get a bit of respite and freedom, members of the family rallied around Dad, and sat with Mum while he went out on the farm, but her health and memory continued to get worse. For Dad, coping with the routine of milking as well as looking after Mum was becoming a great strain, so after some long hard deliberation with Godfrey, they decided the milking and the dairy herd would have to go in favour of Mum's health, and the farm returned to beef rearing.

The sale was arranged for the 30th March 1996 in the Worcester Cattle Market. Dad did not want the sale of the farm; for it was known for visiting farmers and the like to wander around, with thefts taking place during and after sales.

A week before the sale was due to take place the Government news of Mad Cow Disease (BSE) was announced, which threw into crisis the question of whether to abandon or continue the sale.

But it was decided to go ahead. The catalogue was well laid out, giving historic details of each cow and calf, and their milk performance. As a result the herd made good money.

Like most farm enterprises, the countries milk production was on a quota basis to try prevent too much being produced, so this gave the farm the opportunity to sell the quota as well, and in return obtain a beef quota.

Certain paperwork had to be carried out, to show the property was changing its type of operation from dairying to beef.

Soon, through the help of one of the cattle dealers, a small herd of beef cattle were purchased, taking the farm into the next era of business.

Chapter 8

The Changing Seasons

To make a good farmer you have to accept that it is a way of life that you can enjoy rather than making it a career. There is never a spare moment on the farm. When working with animals you start in spring with the lambing, together with twice a day milking and feeding the younger animals. Then in late springtime its time to start planting root crops, potatoes and corn. Haymaking starts in early summer, leading into the harvest of corn followed in autumn by lifting all the roots, potatoes and picking the fruit. In winter most of the cattle will be under cover so they need feeding twice daily. But there are those other jobs like maintaining hedges, which have to be done and do not bring in any money.

Some jobs can be done indoors, like patching corn bags, replacing a spade or axe handle, sorting potatoes, but the majority of jobs have to be done outside, even if it is wet and cold.

There is one country proverb that relates to the weather but is very true, 'Rain before seven, rain till eleven'. If it is raining when you go out to work in the morning, and still raining after breakfast, you can guarantee it will continue to rain most of the morning, but clearing up by lunchtime. If it is still raining at lunchtime, accept the rain will continue all day.

In my young days, there were no plastic coats, trousers or wellingtons to wear. You wore sturdy leather boots, with leggings coming up to just below the knee. If the soul or heal were a bit tired, they would let the water in, soaking your thick 'ullen' (woollen) socks, rapidly letting in the cold. If you were working in the field lifting roots you would wear a sack around your waist, or, if you could afford it, a leather apron. You could wear a long leather coat over your sports jacket, but that would be very heavy. So you would walk up into the granary and acquire an empty Godsell Brown 2.1/2 cwt sack. Taking the one bottom corner you would turn it into the base of the sack until it met the other corner on the inside. You then lifted the turned-in part of the sack over the back of your head, with the width of the sack flowing over your shoulders, and down your back. A piece of binder twine round the waist ensured it stayed in place. You would have to change the bag a couple of times, when the rain continued to pour through the day.

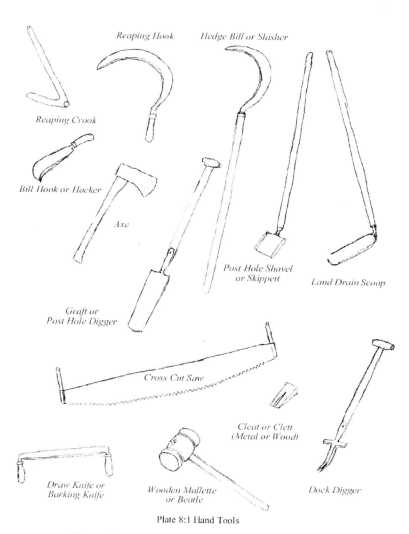

Reaping Hook

Hedge Bill or Slasher

Reaping Crook

Bill Hook or Hacker

Axe

Post Hole Shovel or Skippett

Land Drain Scoop

Graft or Post Hole Digger

Cross Cut Saw

Cleat or Clett (Metal or Wood)

Dock Digger

Draw Knife or Barking Knife

Wooden Mallette or Beatle

Plate 8:1 Hand Tools

The top left hand crook and bill hook were use for cutting corn,
although the bill hook or sickle was used for cutting short grass along the hedge row.
All other tools are used for putting in land drains, wood cutting, fence repairs and hedge laying.

All hedges would need trimming, unless they were getting old and needed re-laying. Using a long handled hedge bill with an upward stroke you would first trim up the sides, striking along the direction of growth to make the cut easy. Trimming the top with a side thrust was more difficult, often having to cut in a downward slant at any larger twigs. You took pride in hedge trimming, cutting the grass alongside and digging the ditch out if there was one leaving a neat tidy job. If you were working along the roadside edge of the field the postman would normally stop and chat as he past by on his bicycle, but when you were hedge trimming his mood would change. He would bitterly protest at the thorns you would be spreading on the road, creating innumerable punctures. So you ensured that you gave the road a good brushing mid-afternoon before he appeared, to appease him and reduce the chance of a puncture.

In Dad's early years, he enjoyed a spot of competition hedge-laying. Unfortunately while hedge-laying, a thorn from a hawthorn branch caught his left eye leaving him partially sighted. When time permits even today he continues to lay hedges. In his 85th year he can still do an excellent job with great skill and agility.

There were only two occasions, while I was still young, that I recall being permitted to join Dad while he was hedge laying. While working along the side of the Dipwood lane that leads up to the Suckley road, he encountered a nest of Adders. Taking the hacker he soon made them into short pieces, showing me for the first time how even after they have been killed they continue to wriggle. The second occasion was along side the lane that leads to Bringsty common, although I was old enough to walk mum had to push me up in a pushchair, having developed a temporary spell of paralysis in the legs which sapped the strength, preventing me from standing or walking for a few days. Hedgerows and fences continually needed maintenance so during winter when no leaves were on the hedges, the gaps would show up, making it easy for any sheep or cattle to make their escape.

Walking along the road in mid July you would notice a bicycle perched up against the roadside hedge, with a builders shovel and heavy broom tied to the cross bar. Each season the County Council employed someone who lived in the village, to trim the embankments, to cut the long grass and foliage that over hung into the road. Once he had trimmed the grass back up under the hedge, he would take the shovel and cut a clean line along the edge, then shovel the loose chippings and soil up onto the embankment.

The roadman knew everyone and was the local newsagent, stopping to talk to everybody that passed by. It was a familiar sight to see the roadman standing with both hands on his shovel. Often you would see the local farmer coming down the road in his Landrover, doing no more than 15 MPH in top gear, with the engine giving out a distinct diesel grunting sound grudgingly trying to keep the vehicle moving. His prime purpose for going so slow was to make sure he kept a good eye on what the neighbouring farmers were doing, and making sure they were not into any other form of farming that would enable them to earn more money than himself. He would pull up alongside the roadman spending anything up to half an hour talking, making sure he got the latest news. Even on the adjacent main road, he would casually pull up, and spend as much time as it took, to glean what information he needed. At times a queue of traffic would be behind waiting to pass getting very irate with him, but he would move on only when he was ready.

Where the fence posts meet the ground, due to the damp and air meeting, rot will set in speedily, so gate posts and fence posts have to be replaced quite regularly .

Dad and John, would set out with the tractor and trailer armed with an axe, wedges, mallet, sledge hammer, length of rope and a cross cut saw, to a well established oak tree, which was found growing in one of the hedge rows. Felling a tree of 100 years old takes a lot of time and sweat. With an axe they first cleaved out a vee around the root bases level with the diameter of the trunk. Then they decided which side they were going to fell it, by cutting a deeper vee slit into what was already cut, to persuade the tree to lean that way. Then they started the laborious task of sawing the tree down using the cross cut saw. With one on each end, squatting on one knee, bend over so that the saw is laying horizontal to the tree as near to the ground as possible. They then started to saw on the opposite side of the trunk from the way you wish it to fall, drawing the saw the full length of the blade at every cut.

The oak is known as the king of the woods for its hardness, and used much for gates, gateposts and fence posts. As the dead wood gets older it continues to harden, so much so that after many years it will become like stone, throwing off sparks as you saw it. Ash is considered to be the queen of the woods, again very strong, used for handles in hand tools, like axes, spades and forks. Burnt ash wood has good lime content and is suitable for the garden. Once the tree was cut down, all the branches and limbs were cut off, cutting the main branches to a suitable length for posts. The trunk was still unmanageable, so the trunk would be split along its length to a suitable size to make gateposts. To split the trunk, you first would use the axe to make a slight indent at the edge of the trunk, then with the help of a 12 lb sledge hammer or beetle drive the sharp end of a steel wedge into the slit to commence splitting. Often before the trunk would start to yield, you would continue to add more wedges along the trunk, and with the aid of the axe, chop into any parts of the split to guide it if the split started to go off course. By the time the trunk begins to split you may have run out of steel wedges, so you improvised with wooden wedges to help finish the job.

In the middle of February 1963 the country experience a very long period of deep frosts, lasting till early April. True the proverb that says. 'As the days lengthen the frosts strengthen'. After the initial down fall of snow, every night we had a very hard frost, which continued to go ever deeper into the ground in more exposed parts up to 2ft 6ins deep. The ice became very thick on the lakes so we took the opportunity to use the ice as a platform, to cut the trees down that lined the side of the lake. Partly to prevent anglers from snagging their lines on them and also to use the wood for fence posts and rails. These trees were called Oral as it was named locally or better known as Alder, growing best near streams or lakes, having a very stringy texture, but very hardy for posts and rails when the bark had been removed. It was much easier to cut and prepared while the sap was still rising, otherwise the wood becomes unmanageable, like cutting strands of wire. Although its very stringy, when freshly cut it is very easy to debark, split and cut to size, before it dries out, leaving your hands and the trunk with a very red, orange stain from the sap.

One of Dad's more favourable tasks was felling trees, which was made much easier with the purchased of his first chain saw. As the trees fell onto the ice, walking around with heavy socks over our boots, which built up a small amount of ice crystals to give grip, we trimmed off the branches and threw the trunks onto

126

the bank. Then we built two fires on top of the ice and burnt all the branches. As heat always rises, together with the build up of ash, we found the ice had hardly melted and that the fires would stay in over the cold night, so we were able to rekindle them easily the next morning.

Mr. Jack Perrigo who was gardener and general handyman at the Gaines told me how after a frosty period the gentry in his younger days would clean off all the leaves on the frozen lake with wide brooms. Then in the early evening after dark the owner of the house would instruct the chauffeur to bring two of the Rolls Royce's down the drive and park one at each corners, at an angle, facing into the centre of the lake. When the guests had arrived, the Rolls Royce's lights were turned on, so they shone across the lake. They would wind up the gramophone that was placed in the centre of the drive between the two cars, turn on the dance music and skate the night away.

Adjacent to the Gaines house was an icehouse with a brick built dovecote overhead. The icehouse comprised of a deep concrete basin let into the ground. In winter the ice was taken from the lake, with layers of meat sat between to act as a refrigerator.

Posts are more vulnerable to rotting at ground level. This is because this area of the post will always be damp. Together the oxygen in the air feeds the damp area at the surface, allowing fungus to set in, enabling the rot to begin. So in order to extend the life of all fencing materials they will be immersed in creosote. The bark is soft and will retain moisture, remaining damp and allowing rot to set in. An axe or a double-ended cleaver is used to trim off all the bark from posts and rails. Some farms had a brick built creosote tank with a fireplace underneath to pickle the posts and aid the absorption time. We improvised using a large 40-gallon oil barrel, with the one end cut out. A small amount of creosote would be poured into the bottom, and then filled with the posts. Till the creosote stopped being absorbed the tank would be kept topped up, as the creosote soaked into the wood. Then the posts were turned over and the process repeated on the other end. As the rails were too long to dip they would be creosoted by hand with a brush.

As well as being gardener for the Gaines, Jack Perrigo spent quite a lot of time working on the farm gaining much knowledge to the layout of the farm. His knowledge of where all the water pipes ran under ground proved invaluable, having seen them being laid originally. The first sets of water pipes were in lead, carrying water from a spring in the windmill field. The soil had been cleared from around the spring to reveal a platform of rock, with a 3inch jagged slit in the centre up which the water fed. Around it a brick wall was built with a concrete roof and a steel manhole cover. In early days the spring had a windmill on top, which pumped the water to a reservoir, on the upper most point of the field, and then was piped by gravity to the Gaines house. Occasionally the water would reduce to a trickle so Jack Perrigo with a pressure pump would attach it to the pipe near to the spring and blasted out a 6-inch long spongy weed that lived and thrived along the length of pipe.

During the long frost of 1963, the pipeline regularly froze, particularly where it was not too deep in the ground or where the snow had been cleared on the driveway to the farm. The local blacksmith Jack Roberts hired out his electric welder as a means of thawing the pipes along the farm driveway. A hole was dug part way up the driveway, and another at the bottom of the drive near to the cowshed. Some pieces of old metal pipe were joined together, and laid above ground along the line of the water pipe. At the top end of the yard one piece of cable was used to connect the underground pipeline to the old line of pipes. At the bottom of the drive the old pipe was joined to the welder. Another piece of cable leading from the welder was joined to the underground pipe to make a circuit. By turning the power on it acted in the same manner as an electric fire. The circuit passing through the water pipe warmed the water, and as soon as the water started to flow, the water itself aided the speed of melting. We were able to carry out this method of getting water for some days but as the freeze up continued to bite, the frost crept across the fields where it was difficult to detect, so it meant having to carry the water from the spring with a three point lift box on the back of the tractor. Each day loaded with six churns and a length of string attached to a steel bucket we headed for the reservoir making two or three trips before all the animals and the farm house were satisfied. The sun shone gloriously over the bright hard, snow-covered ground, making travelling easy. John would let down the bucket into the tank, and I transferred the bucket of water into the churns.

When ice thaws it expands and the water pipes have no give in the steel material, so with it came the inevitable leaks. Leaks would occur both on the outside taps and inside the sheds with joints springing apart everywhere. Any weak rusty underground joints would also show up with water coming up out of the ground in unexpected places along the line of the pipe, forming a small stream.

Plate 8:2 Dad laying hedge

Hubert now living in the one bungalow, had little experience of tractor work, but he did have a good understanding of farming and a good knowledge of working with animals. We soon discovered that Marg was a most efficient and professional worker to the envy of the farmers in the village able to do any job that was given her to do,. She was fast and conscientious with every task she did, with singling roots, potato planting and sorting, with fruit picking to name a few. She was renowned for having the ability to accurately adjudge weights, fill her cherry basket, damson box or potato bag, and not have to add or take any off when they were put on the scales.

Marg had a Jack Russell dog called 'Poppet'. Poppet accompanied Hubert most of the time while working on the farm.

One of the non-productive activities in mid-july was cutting the nettles, docks and thistles that would grow profusely in clumps around the farmyard, and in the fields and orchards where the sheep and cattle were grazing.

There is a farming proverb which says. 'Cut them in June, they will come again soon, cut them in July, they will be sure to die'. This proverb is true, so under orders from Dad I would attach the side cut bar mower to Dolly the Fordson Major and spend some days cutting the rubbish as we termed it around the fields and orchards. Where ever there are fruit trees, its difficult to cut all the weeds against the tree so these had to be cut by hand. One morning Hubert brought along Poppet with him to cut the surplus thistles on the field called the Old Bath. Hubert with hedge bill over his shoulder had shut the field gate, and was approaching the tractor from behind, to begin cutting the nettles around a small plantation of damson trees. Over the noise of the tractor engine I heard the shrill whistle of Hubert calling the dog, to turn and see Poppet running toward the mower knife. Before I had time to stop the machine, Poppet had run over the moving blade missing the cutter bar with his front feet, but nicking the tendons of his back legs. Before I could get my breath, Hubert had picked up his dog, and was making a hasty retreat back to the farm. When I went home for lunch I was to discover that Hubert had asked Dad to take Poppet straight to the vet, where he put a few stitches in the back of each leg, with great protests from the dog. I got the impression that Hubert was feeling sorer than Poppet afterwards, after Marg had described what she thought of him, when he returned home.

Cows will eat some of the thistles and nettles, when the plants had wilted, yet cutting rubbish reminds me of the farmer who wanted to find an easy way of getting rid of his thistles. During a conversation with one farmer friend, he was pleased to hear that donkeys ate thistles. So loosing no time he bought a donkey and put him into the field where most of the thistles were growing. After a couple of weeks he kept a close eye on the donkey, but the thistles did not get less, in fact they kept growing. He left it a couple of weeks longer, but still no change. Now totally confused and despondent, he contacted the farmer who had recommended the donkey. In an assertive way the farmer asked, "Has the donkey eaten all the grass?" "No!" replied the distraught farmer.

"Then wait till he has eaten all the grass he'll be glad to eat the thistles".

During the summer of 1976 Britain experienced a severe drought lasting from July into the middle of September. The grass in all the fields turned yellow, from lack of water, with the farmer having to feed their animals on the next winters stored feed. Many of the brooks dried up, which was the only source of drink for cattle grazing on streamside meadows. In some parts of Wales, farmers were using JCB buckets on the end of the hydraulic jib to try and reach the underground springs. But when the man made springs dried, they ended up using their slurry tankers for transport, to carry water from adjacent rivers, taking up a lot of the farmers' valuable time.

Back home the Snygmore reservoir got so low that the water line fell four foot below the culvert top, where it was pumped up to the reservoir. During the three-month drought the water line fell four foot below the culvert where the petrol pump drew the water. So we had to use Dolly the tractor, the Fordson Major Diesel KFD with a Power Take Off pump on the back, to pump the water over the reservoir wall into the culvert, so the petrol pump could do its job. The lake in front of the house, started to get a covering of green algae, and began to loose oxygen. Fish started to die and float on the surface, so we had to hire a water pump, creating a fountain in the centre of the lake, to allow the air to oxygenate the water, as it sprayed into the air.

Chapter 9

Home Life

Mum's desire was for each of her five children to be born at the farm. I was the first to be born, but during birth, the midwife became concerned and realised I was causing Mum some difficulty. It was coming up to midnight, yet she felt she had to call the doctor out from Bromyard, some four miles away. On arrival the doctor indicated that the difficulty was caused by my head positioned slightly out of line to my body, and had to admit that to correct the situation was beyond his skills. So very apologetically he called for an ambulance and had us quickly admitted to Worcester Infirmary. The birth proved to be quite an ordeal, and quite distressing for both Mum and myself. Within the first couple of months I had developed an ulcerated mouth infection. Dad had to prise my lips open to get the bottle into my mouth to feed me, for the infection was sticking my lips together. Penicillin was available and would have healed my mouth, but could only be administered in a hospital; so back in I had to go, for another week.

Sometime later, due to falling and cutting my lip I suddenly got a bad attack of Eczema, which fled all over my body, so again, I was back into hospital, having to be washed in paraffin. The Eczema stayed with me right into adult life, but only in small patches, over the top of my hands. Unceremoniously the top of the fingers would split open in any cold or damp weather, yet having been wrapped in Elastoplasts for a day, it would heal as quick as it came. The main discomforts of eczema were the way it would itch, at times causing me to scratch the skin until the flesh became red raw and at times bleed. Eczema is a condition that affects the nerve endings. Some of the healthy nerves are unaffected close by, but when you scratch the itchy area there is a conflict between the infected nerves that are very itchy and the healthy nerves which begin to sting and become sore with the constant scratching. Over the years innumerable ointments have been offered to me, but with little effect. At present, only Sudocrem is able to relieve it, but in an emergency applying saliva to your skin is good first aid. I was a very nervous child, living under very strict christian ethics of my father, so any form of stress would soon cause the Eczema to flare up, often giving me a lot of discomfort particularly at night when I was tired before my body settled down for sleep.

Plate 9:1 The Townsend family 1954

I was a very anxious and insecure child, getting little support outside the family unit spending much of my time finding my own way. I was very nervous when asked to speak to an adult, or if they approached me. I would feel tense in any stressful situations, right into adult life, which made the eczema flare up many times. During one short spell in later life when I had job security, and a nucleus of rich friends and feeling very happy in myself the eczema disappeared completely for a short while then I was made redundant from my first job, then the Eczema returned and has stayed with me to this day. During those early years I developed a fear of darkness, and danger. There had been a number of plane crashes, making it very difficult to get to sleep at night. Planes regularly seemed to be passing over the farmhouse at night making me fearful every time one droned over head, expecting them to dive down and crash into the house. To overcome my phobia dad purchased a transformer which fitted into the light socket, with a bulb that gave off a very low light, which stayed on all night bringing some comfort to me till I grew older, and stronger in spirit.

133

Memories of my young childhood are very sparse. It is said that when our recollection of a certain period of our life has been blotted out, it is due to times of unhappiness. I do recall good times with Dad, while with him working in the fields, like hedging and sowing grass seed by hand, counting the sheep, pruning the fruit trees, helping plant the potatoes, and lifting them. I would go in the car to the local market, and while travelling to sheep sales in Wales, hear him explain all the different aspects of farming to me. In the spring he would take me to Knightwick railway station to pick up a fresh batch of new day old chicks.

We had very few toys, when we were younger, and never ever recall Dad or Mum engaging in any of the pleasures with us. Admirably we would receive storybooks, and placards with bible verses, for Christmas presents, and Sunday school prizes. We were told how detrimental television was to view, but listening to anything on the radio was all right.

As a young family, we made friends with other parents, who we met during the school term. Then during holiday periods, we had the opportunity to invite our school friends' back to play, but sadly, only on very rare occasions, was I allowed to do so. It was great, on the odd occasion to visit friends whose children had toys to play with, but alas, at home, with few toys, having to find your own amusement, it often resulted in having arguments with my brother Paul. Because of mum's obsessive fear of water dad put up a 6 ft high fence adjacent to the house, to protect us from the lake, that becoming our playtime territory. Occasionally we were allowed out into the farmyard area, but only to fetch items for mum, such as wood for the fire, potatoes or apples for dinner.

When we were old enough we were given a toy tractor, a car and a jeep that we could sit on and pedal along. Dad also made a trailer out of a fruit box and some pram wheels, which enabled us the opportunity of fetching logs for the fire, from the barn close to the house. During the summer we could venture into the farmyard to get the wood, stumbling over the very uneven cobbled yard, but we were spending more time having to get off the tractor seat, waddling our feet on the ground and dragging the tractor or car out of the ruts, until the single front wheel of the tractor collapsed. The wheel arch was brazed back making it a little more sturdy.

In the winter driving the toy car and tractor was a little more pleasure, because we were allowed to make a corridor through the house, opening up all the doors through the lounge, hall and granny kitchen, until Mum got fed up with the cold draught from all the doors being open.

A Christmas never went by without Father Christmas leaving one of Dad's large socks filled with an orange, apple, banana and a few sweets.

I would get loads of sweets each Christmas, but I was just not interested. For Paul who slept in the same room as me, found it far different, he just loved them. I would take the large tin that I first received when visiting Cadbury's factory, and added the sweets to the ever-growing store, and there they would stay till the next Christmas. It was some years before I came to realise that to give them to other children was a polite gesture. One year we had a torch and did enjoy reading under the blanket, after Dad had put the light out, till the battery ran out. Asking for a new battery would be seen as a financial crisis, so we were not allowed a fresh one. Having a torch had little point for after all, going out side at night for us was unheard of.

I recall when quite young, Mum taking me to visit an elderly lady in Bromyard. I can remember the black long attire, and high lace up boots. On leaving the ladies home she would produce a bag of black coloured sweets, and offer me one. Being nervous and shy, I had to take one and dared not refuse to eat it putting it straight into my mouth. But the taste was vile and awful to devour, but I felt obliged to eat it.

When I started at the Whitbourne village junior school, I was always forgetting to take the dinner money to school on Friday morning, so Dad came up with a solution. He got an empty Corn Flake packet and cut the one side out to make a large circle. On the inside of the packet he wrote in large bold lettering Dinner Money 3/9d. and stuck it on the wall in the dining room. It solved the problem for a time, until we got used to not noticing it.

On arrival at school in winter, when the snow had fell, it was a treat to watch the Collins family sportingly creating an ice slide and with great rhythm and a steady foot slide down the slopping school playground, stopping against the rugged stonewall, separating us from the road.

Miss Pitt, the head mistress was always well dressed, especially in winter. On time, a few minutes before lessons she would appear from the schoolhouse adjacent, mostly with a

135

beaming smile showing her large set of teeth, and walk briskly across the playground wearing a long thick coat with a scarf of mink skin wrapped around her neck. As she was of Scottish descent she would often be wearing a thick tartan jacket and skirt.

If Dad had managed to get us to school a few minutes early, every week day morning strictly at 9–30am Miss Pitt would come out onto the entrance steps of the school and blow the whistle loudly.

After getting into line in pairs, we would troop up the three sets of steps to the front of the senior classroom. Morning assembly began with all the pupils standing and singing a hymn, accompanied by Mrs Brodie the junior teacher sitting at the piano. Then Miss Pitt followed on by taking a bible reading and saying a prayer. If Mrs Brodie was not there Miss Pitt would use her tuning fork to strike the right note, then with a short conductors stick, she quite professionally led us. We the junior class would troop through the back entrance hall, through the dining kitchen into our own classroom.

Mrs Brodie, was the wife to one to one of our neighbours. She had all the hallmarks of a farmers wife, strong built and having a very deep gruff voice, which I later learnt would have been used with much force at home, yet at school she was a good teacher very caring and sensitive.

Once we got to our places after morning assembly, Mrs Brodie would open by saying *"Good morning children"*, and we would dutifully respond, *"Good morning Mrs Brodie."* It was now time to get down to some serious work.

Each one of us had a small blackboard edged with a wooden frame, using white chalk to write with. If we were doing any modelling plastercene would be used, getting rolled up many times in the palms of the hands until we could get it right. When it came to reading we had the various aspects of farm life portrayed on the walls, including Mr. Plod the policeman. As still happens even today, mid morning and again mid-afternoon we had playtime. Even today, it still brings a soft hearty warm glow to my heart and happy memories of junior school days when I hear the children laughing and shouting in any school playground.

Just before the end of the last afternoon session, after ensuring we had cleared everything away we would all have to stand and repeat the Lord's prayer, after which we were immediately dismissed and allowed to run off home.

All the parents would meet at the school gate, including David Gines's mum, one of the mother's who lived at the lodge connected to Whitbourne Hall. She always had to bring their little terrier dog with her, so that he could have the thrill of sitting on the cross bar of David's bicycle with his two front paws on the handle bar and have a ride home.

During the hot summer days, walking from school down the hill on our journey home, we would try and persuade Mum to give us some money and treat us to an ice cream. We were allowed to go into the local pub and purchase the ice-cream from Mrs. Linington, who lived in and ran the pub. This was one of two pubs in the village, standing on the corners of where the village lane met the A44 main road to Bromyard. As you walked down the hill to the pub, David Gines would come flying down the road, with both hands free, and his terrier dog sitting happily on the cross bar. During the summer we would soon pass David's home to see him steadily walking behind a two-wheeled Atco grass mower. I would watch David using this machine so confidently, needing only to walk behind it as young as was, wishing dad had the same make of machine at home so I could be given the chance and opportunity to use one, instead of the Autoculto which Dad had to run behind, to keep up with.

When we were old enough and moved up into Miss Pitt's top class, David was not amiss at causing a little excitement. Miss Pitt would have given us 20 minutes of teaching on a subject and then we would be set some writing on the subject. All would soon settle into a nice quiet time, except for the desk top occasionally being dropped shut or a wooden ruler bumped on a desk. At her desk, which was quite bare except for her course wooden cane and a sharp penknife that got used frequently to sharpen our pencils, Miss Pitt would be attending to one of the pupils.

While everyone had their heads down, unbeknown to the class, David while still writing with his right hand would stretch out his left leg and place his cupped hand under the back of the knee below his short legged trousers. Suddenly he would draw his foot back up closing around the clasped hand, which gave out a large raspy noise like the wind being let out of a balloon.

Miss Pitt would instantly and silently look up unable to know what to say, and not knowing who did it, except for the class, would just glare with lips tightly clasp.

For the rest of us who guessed the culprit we were also tight lipped, while our tummies were trembling like jellies taking great pains not to titter.

Plate 9:2 Front of Farmhouse with outside toilet

For many years David's father George, supplied us with his own home baked bread. But when he retired, we took our business to Wheal and Bakeman's of Bromyard.

During holiday time, Paul and I, when wandering the farm yard, would keep a wary eye and ear for the twice weekly bread van coming up the road, or get an early warning from the dogs barking, and the tinny sound of the van's body racing over the drive ruts, and hastily reversing down to the farmhouse door. Immediately we heard the van we would race down the yard, with our feet hardly touching the ground to arrive by the van, just as the baker was opening the rear doors, as mum gazed in to make her selection. The aroma of freshly baked bread coming from the inside of the van will be a lasting memory. Mum would get quite a selection of loaves together with perhaps a malt loaf, and a few doughnuts, then drop them into his large wicker basket for the baker to courteously carry back to the farmhouse. At this point, Paul and I are silently holding our breath to see if Mum was going to give us our treat, but the baker, knowing we both liked and wanted a marsh mellow each, would not miss a chance to make an extra sale, so with Mum's permission, he would hand us one each. We would happily tuck in to the treat and run off to play to await the baker's next visit.

As we neared the end of our time at the junior school, Miss Pitt asked me if I would like to help her father with the gardening. This was the common practice for all the older pupils. I was keen as mustard to get away from Miss Pitt's strictness and outside in the fresh air and on a sunny day, away from closed doors of the classroom.

Mr. Pitt dressed in a light brown apron and had quite a stern character, but was very pleasant, well able to show and teach you what had to be done. Carrying a hoe he would wheel out his wooden barrow up to the flower border against the school wall, , and start to demonstrate which were the weeds and begin pulling them up out of the rich loamy soil into the wheelbarrow. I would then have to wheel the barrow to the top of the playground through the back gate, across the road to the old pond and dump the weeds on its edge. My next task was to lightly fork the very amiable soil, while Mr. Pitt spread a liberal amount of blood and bone meal, raking it in as he spread it.

Each season he would have lifted the Primulus flowers in late spring and put them into a nursery and then replant them back again in the autumn ready for the next showing. I gained quite a lot of valuable knowledge from working out in the school gardens.

Monday morning was and still is the traditional day for washing. While I was quite young, Mum would bucket soft rainwater from the outside tank, and tip it into the large boiler that was in the outhouse, at the entrance to the farmhouse just outside the kitchen. While the water was boiling up, she would be working at the kitchen sink, soaking any shirt collars that had got engrained with dirt and sweat. In went the garments and once the boiler had finished boiling up the clothes, she would occasionally pull out a garment, throwing a few flakes of washing powder on it, and set about scrubbing it between her hand, to get any difficult stains out. She would then take the tongues and transfer the boiling hot washing into a metal tub alongside. Once the washing was cool enough to handle she would rinse them out by hand, and place them in a washing basket. Picking up the washing basket, she would make her way out to the mangle that was strategically placed over the drain and standing just outside the outhouse. Taking the first item of washing in her left hand, she would turn the handle of the top roller, which propelled the lower roller by a gear on the lower side, squeezing the garment between the two rollers, as the surplus water gushed down into the drain. The washing was now ready for hanging out on the line.

Mid week, around mid-morning every Wednesday the grocery representative from Shutter and Flay's in Worcester would arrive to take our order, to be delivered the following Friday. While happily tucking into a cup of coffee, and some home made farmhouse cake, he would unceremoniously break into the familys' conversation, to add his opinions. He would spend up to two hours talking and well able to keep a conversation going, with Dad treating him to an awful lot of leg pulling torment. Then much to everyone's relief, he would suggest that it was time he was on his way. He would then take out of his pocket a small notebook, making a note of our name and the date. Then Mum would quickly recite all the items she needed in rapid succession, taking no more than five minutes, and before he had the book back in his pocket he was up and away. With the grocery rep turning up it was a reminder to Mum to telephone the butcher with our order for meat, to be delivered on the following Saturday.

On Friday every one turned up to deliver their goods, the baker, and the grocer. Pettifer's of Bromyard would also turn up fairly regularly to supply hardware goods, as would Dairy Supplies of Hereford, to see if Dad needed any spare items for the dairy.

Dad's days were very long, for, as we have discovered farming is not a job of work, more a way of life. Even when the day is finished, most evenings he would be outside, feeding the dogs, sorting fruit or potatoes, doing that odd job to make things go smoother the next day. With a family of five Mum's day was just as busy. But at whatever time of day visitors arrived Mum would always give them a hearty welcome. As you approached the farmhouse door way you would be met by the smell of warm baking and cooking. Most days you would find Mum in the kitchen with a flowery cotton apron around her waist standing

140

along side the dining table with her hands and arms deep inside a mixing bowl. Often I would watch her kneading butter between her fingers, mixing it with the flour preparing a cake for cooking, while listening to a large pot on the cooker quietly bubbling away making plum or damson jam. There were as yet no freezers available to buy, so in summer she would be splicing beans and ramming them into large jars together with layers of salt to use over the winter months. Any leftover potatoes, fish or meat from dinner, would be rolled into cakes to fry. The left overs from a chicken would be boiled up for broth. Regularly Dad would kill a chicken, and mum would immediately get it in the long shallow china sink, and pluck it while it is still warm. Then getting a burning roll of news paper, she would draw the flaming paper over its body to burn off all the soft down, finally cutting off the head, and take out the intestines. Often someone would turn up with a wild rabbit, which she would take little time to skin and draw the innards or intestines. When a pig was killed there was little that was not used. There was the pig's head, the feet or trotters, that were boiled, and then any left overs were again made into broth.

The moments of time Mum had to relax, particularly in the evenings, she would occupy her time mending socks, or putting a patch on some trousers, then would keep busy sewing up a new garment on the treadle Singer sewing machine or knitting socks, scarf or gloves. I would be roped into sitting opposite her, with outstretched arms with skeins of wool, that is the wool in a wrap about 2 ft in diameter, while Mum wound it into a ball, in readiness for knitting. If we had surplus milk from the house cow, I would sit turning the handle of the butter churn, patiently waiting for the lumps of butter to form. It needed 10 gallons of milk to make 1Lb. of butter. Surplus milk was also made into junket, using milk, which had been warmed with a little sugar, rennet and nutmeg added, and then allowed to set like jelly. Junket was a beautiful tasty dessert on a hot summers day, when eaten cold.

She often reminded us that living in a black and white house meant a lot of hard work. All the exposed beams collected a good deal of dust, caused by the crumbling mortar between, and the old wattle and daub that constantly needed re-plastering. Mum liked to take a paintbrush and redden up the fireside hearth, or give the beams a coat of black paint, occasionally lifting the stair rods and giving the side of the stairway steps a coat.

Plate 9:3 Rear entrance of Farmhouse

We could not afford to buy carpets, so she would cut up strips of cotton cloth and weave them into hessian sacking to make rag carpets. In the very early days Mum went to work in one of the local hop yards, but when I started going to the secondary school, a neighbour who owned a carpet shop in Worcester asked if she would help him to make rugs from old carpet off cuts, and enabled us to get some cheap carpets. In winter he also employed Mum to transfer hop string from large skeins into smaller balls, to make it easier to carry around in the hop yards.

In late summer Mum also went over to the neighbouring farm to help with the black currant picking. I went along with her in the school holidays to get my hands on real money for the first time, enabling me to buy things for myself. You picked the blackberries into 6 or 12Lb baskets, and then transferred them into 20Lb trays. At the end of the day the farmer weighed each tray, recording the weights in a book that you kept with you. At the end of the first week after having the last tray weighed, I received my first pay packet, trotting off home feeling very proud and wealthy. Later that evening I went to pick up the wage packet to take to my bedroom, but when I came to the desk in the dining room, where I thought I had left the wage packet, it was missing. I was beside myself, dashing around asking if anyone had seen it. After tea mum told me to think back to where I had been, and promised they would go along with me to trace my footsteps, which included walking across some of the fields on the farm. So we did that, but failed to find it. For the next few days I regularly scouted over the places that I thought I had been, but eventually had to put it out of my mind, and get back to the blackberry patch to earn another packet. From then on I kept the money in my pocket for safety.

At Christmas and on birthdays it was not the custom in our family to give one another cards, but this particular year when I came downstairs on the morning of my birthday I had such a surprise, for there on the dining room table, where I sat to eat, was the pay packet I had lost. Well I started to ask questions, to discover that everyone in the house had conspired to hide the pay packet, and keep it till my birthday. I took it in good part, but other friends thought it a very mean joke to play on me.

Animals need feeding seven days a week. Sundays were strictly observed as a day of rest, apart from the feeding times, yet for us it was one of the busiest days of the week. Dad changed the business over to dairying, just after my thirteenth birthday. Although most of the farm worker finished mid-day on the Saturday, the assistant milker had to have his regular weekends off, as well as his annual holidays. Although I was not old enough to leave school I was expected to spend a good deal of my weekend leisure time helping out.

Early Sunday morning, started with fetching the cows in and helping with the milking. Dad and I would rarely exchange conversation, only to be told what to do next, or be told in a gruff charismatic tone what I had done wrong or what I had not done. Breakfast time, we were able only to snatch a bite to eat, often leaving the cowshed floor in a mess after milking, I would jump into the van, as Dad sped off up the yard to deliver the milk around the local villages.

In the mid 1960's the farm landlord decided to sell the large mansion that stood at the rear of the farmhouse. I was now in my fourteenth year, Reg and Audrey Lawrence, the new custodians who were going to live in the property, and oversee the work as a Bible Teaching Centre, came over to meet Dad, introducing themselves as Evangelical Christians. They explained that the new trustees, had run into difficulties raising the deposit, and that the sale would fall through, if the full deposit was not met by a certain date. Dad was able to put them in touch with a Christian financier, who agreed to forward a loan to secure the property.

Daily I had to deliver milk to the mansion house, having to climb a steep set of stairs at the rear of the mansion up to the first floor, soon getting to know the family very well. It was not long before I was being invited back over to their home in the evenings, always to be met with a warm welcome and greeted like a long lost friend.

Each Sunday morning, because I was not old enough to drive, Audrey drove the van and chauffeured me around the villages, while I delivered the bottled milk, giving Dad time to finish the work in the dairy, and get ready for the early morning service at the chapel, Through these daily visits to the mansion, and Audrey's generous help on a Sunday, it allowed Audrey to share with me some of the intimate heart aches, criticisms and difficulties they were having, setting up of the work at Gaines. I began to spend most of the little spare time I had with the Lawrence family. They gave me valuable help in my Christian living, showing me direction and teaching me new values to life, which proved of immense importance in later years.

Dad would have the once a week chance to dress in his best suit, polishing his shoes till you could see your face in them. At the last minute after a frantic rush around the kitchen to comb his hair, he would dash out through the door facing the lake, along the clean garden path so as to avoid steeping out the other side of the house into the mucky farmyard, taking a short cut up the side of the stable yard to the top barn where he garaged the car. He would have to hastily pick his way through the mud up the last part of the farm drive, and open the large double doors of the barn, which had a large clasp, that would give a metallic ring as it fell open. As you walked into the barn you would notice a large tarpaulin slung over the car, to stop the birds leaving their calling cards on his gleaming Ford 8 car. This was his first car and he would often reminded us of how he bought the car for £100 and some years later was able to sell it for the same money. His next car was a Morris 12.

During the working week the animals would behave well, due to the workmen being around, but Sundays, they seemed to know

Dad or anybody else was not around, for they got into all sorts of trouble. The bull would pick up the scent and voice of a cow that was in season, and find his way out and into the next farmers herd. Often one of our cows would venture too far into the pond to get water, and get well bogged down in the mud. Another cow picking up the smell of ripe apples, would find a hole in the hedge, push through and gorge herself.

One Sunday one of the neighbouring farmers rang Mum to tell her the bull was in his cattle. Fortunately the family who lived at the farm next to the chapel were owner of the cattle transport business that we used, and members of the chapel. Mum rang the farm next to the chapel, then one member of the family had to go into the service and bring Dad out, taking home one of the workmen, who was also in the service.

To get the amorous bull away from the neighbours' cows and back home meant every one being asked to help taking with them a pitch fork, to ensure the bull understood that he had to go back home. Fetching the cows out of the orchard was a little easier, and after the bull had returned, it always meant mending the fence, to prevent them returning through the same gap again. Occasionally as the result of getting into the orchard one of the cows would get a small apple caught part way down her throat, closing up the windpipe. So the vet would have to come out, but more often than not just by pushing the apple into her stomach with a probe solved the problem. One Sunday soon after one of the cows got into the orchard she began to get very unsteady on her feet. Once the gang had managed to coax her home, the vet again was called. After getting to know the facts and making the cow wobble around the field for a few moments, he smiled and said "She's only drunk, she will get over it". Getting a cow out of the pond needed more careful planning. In early days, sometimes one of the Shire horses got stuck, and needed a long rope and two more horses, using a rope and pulley's commonly referred to as a block and tackle. When the rope is anquored to a tree, you get much better pulling power. When a cow gets stuck you may have to lay a ladder on the mud to walk across, and put a rope round the horns, neck or belly, then use a tractor to tow her out.

As soon as Audrey and I had returned from delivering the milk, I would dash into the farmhouse to get changed and race back into the car and off with dad to the morning service. Mum rarely went

145

to the morning service at the chapel, unless we had some visiting Christian friend staying with us, then we all had to go.

Plate 9:4 Paul and David collecting logs for the fire

Sunday lunchtime did have its lighter moments. When Godfrey and Gordon, my younger brothers, were around eight and nine years of age they formed a strong bond together, always tormenting one another or teasing someone else. You would regularly hear Gordon crying out in protest, because Godfrey was tormenting him, eventually keeping Godfrey at arms length until he quietened down a little. During the lunch hour Godfrey would discretely slide onto the floor, and quietly tie both my shoes together with the shoelaces, or tie my shoelaces to Paul's shoes. Then if Godfrey was not tormenting us boys, he would go round the back of his mum, and undo the laces on her pinafore, with the pinafore immediately falling round her feet when she stood up. If that were not enough, he would take off her spectacles, claiming they wanted cleaning. Then using the dishcloth to wipe them, leaving a greasy film on the lenses. If Godfrey caught mum in the chair having a sleep after getting the dinner, he would get some small paper reinforcing rings and gently stick then on the lenses of her specs, to look like Noddy with two telescopes, much to the amusement of everyone else. Once dinner was over, I would have to change back into my working clothes to clean the cowshed down from the early morning milking.

During the afternoon in summer you could get an hours respite from work, but in winter time the rest of the day was hectic. All the animals would need their second feeding, which meant driving the tractor and trailer up to the various fields with feed. Even before I had a licence to drive, dad would drive the tractor and trailer into the field. Having set the tractor in a low, slow gear, he would hand over to me to carry on steering, then he would jump onto the trailer, and shovel out either mangolds, sugar beet tops, Swedes or wads of hay. You also needed to make sure all the animals had adequate amounts of water, which meant a large number of journeys to and from the water tank with a water bucket in either hand. Then they needed to have a liberal amount of fresh straw brought and shaken up for their bedding. At 2-45pm meant a quick dash back to the farmhouse and back into your best clothes, then leaping into the back of the van and off to Sunday school, stopping to pick children up on the way. Arriving back home from Sunday school at around 4-30pm after a long diversion to take the children back home, it was back into my old clothes again to fetch the cows from the field, for the second milking. Because I was so tired from the long arduous Sunday work, I would often start to doze on the way to and from Sunday school. The afternoon milking became a painful episode because I was so tired. On the back cowshed wall there was a recess or hatch with a door in it, used to throw the manure out into the bottom yard. Whenever a spare moment came, particularly on a Sunday I would flop down into the hatch leaning back against the sidewall to get a nap, till Dad called me to usher the next group of cows into the parlour. Once the milking was finished the cowshed floor was left unclean again, and I, often with only a drink and a bite of a biscuit to eat, would dive back into the house to get changed yet again, to dash

147

off to the evening service. I can often remember started to doze off during the service, creaking my neck, then suddenly jumping and coming to, feeling quite embarrassed hoping no one had noticed me sleeping. Once back home, I was back again into my working clothes to clean the cowshed, by which time I was more than ready for bed. By now it was 8-30pm, so with a mug of coffee in one hand, and a beef dripping sandwich in the other I was off to bed, only too aware that I had a bus to catch for school at 8-15am the next morning.

When we had a fall of snow it was a great delight for us when very young to get our wellingtons on and build a snowman, utilising some of the lumps of coal from the shed for his eyes and buttons, then getting a small twig for his mouth and nose. When we were older, we would have no time during the day to play, because we would be busy, carrying kettles of hot water to thaw taps, getting our pleasure out of seeing the water start to flow. But when evening came, and the moon was full out we would make our way up to the Windmill field for some sledging. We would put a few extra layers on because it would be below freezing, making the snow more crisp, and easier to sledge down. We would pull our trousers outside our wellingtons, to prevent the snow slipping inside building up into a matt of ice between our warm legs and the outside of the wellington, and preventing our feet getting very cold.

Up the road we would trudge with one towing a sledge, another carrying the large shovel from the corn bin, while another would be dragging a large plastic fertiliser bag stuffed with straw. With two riding the sledge at a time was great fun, till you met a ridge in the ground. Soon the sledge began dipping and surging until it came to a halt wedged in the snow. Then the rear of the sledge would fly into the air continue on down the slope as Paul and I started to somersault, and pitch poll over and over as great shouts of laughter came from all standing by. The down side was pulling the sledge back up the bank again.

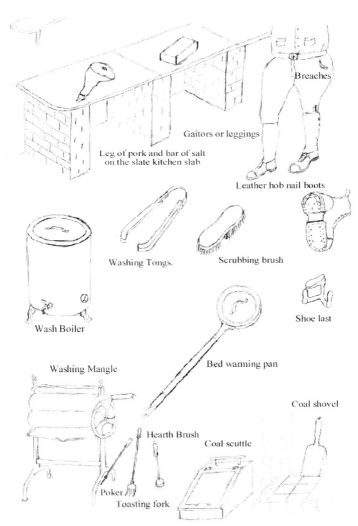

Breaches

Gaitors or leggings

Leg of pork and bar of salt
on the slate kitchen slab

Leather hob nail boots

Washing Tongs.

Scrubbing brush

Shoe last

Wash Boiler

Bed warming pan

Washing Mangle

Coal shovel

Hearth Brush

Coal scuttle

Poker

Toasting fork

Plate 9:5 Items that live in the farmhouse

149

The shovel had to be used with great skill and agility. One of us would squat on the shovel base, with both hands taking a firm grip facing the handle. Then if the shovel did not start to move by itself, someone gave you a shove, but it was not long before the centre of gravity changed and the shovel started to spin round, with you doing a waltz, hanging on for dear life till you lost your balance and finally tumbled off.

The fertiliser bag was a little easier and gentler to use, but the layer of soft straw was not sufficient to prevent you from feeling all the lumps and bumps on your bottom as you sailed over the frozen snow.

Until we had the dairy unit installed we had no proper sanitation. Upstairs on the balcony, we had a small square framework made out of plasterboard to use as a toilet with a free standing Elsan Closet inside. The Elsan Closet comprised of a large cylindrical container with a plastic toilet seat and cover, with a deep bucket placed inside to catch the business. After each time the bucket was emptied Dad would pour a small amount of water in, and add a measure of Jayes fluid. Once the toilet was full, which amounted to at least once a week, depending on the rate the family was growing, dad would have to carry the bucket down stairs to the area next to the pool, dig a substantially deep hole and pour the contents in and earth it back up. There was another Elson toilet in a little black corrugated outhouse outside, at the far end of the farmhouse. For obvious reasons it was not used much in winter, yet it was quite a convenient retreat, for as a big family you could get away for some much needed peace and quiet. In those early days the rolls of toilet paper were of a dark brown colour, but with a texture as slick as greaseproof paper, and little absorption ability. We relished using sheets of news paper, which had been ripped up into small wads, and forced over the end of a nail, hammered into the door post.

The log fire in the lounge was the only form of heat in the house, so we had to boil water on the electric cooker to have our morning wash. Using one of the first safety razors, with the double-edged blades Dad would make claim to the warm water first to have his after-breakfast shave and wash. He would have his shave over the large deep china kitchen sink in the kitchen. In front was a small window hinged from the bottom, and could be opened from the top about 45 deg. back into the kitchen. In the early days, Jack Perrigo's daughter, while in her teens, would daily come and visit the farm. She enjoyed working with the animals, confidently fetching in the Shire horses, for feeding. Joyce was a lady of fun and often-teased Dad, yet he would be a match for her. She had a longhaired terrier called Mickey, which Dad delighted in tormenting. Each time Joyce endeavoured to set off for home, Dad would start to call the terrrier back, to which he would dutifully respond as Joyce sought to call him back. One morning while Dad was shaving Joyce was making fun at Dad through the kitchen window. Once Dad had finished shaving, instead of pouring the water down the sink, he discretely lifted up the bowl of shaving water, and gently let the water rush down over the glass of the open window. The water came out at such an angle that it caught Joyce just below the chin well washing her chest. In future she kept her distance when tormenting dad while shaving.

If and when it was decided that we were due to have a bath, which seemed to get less frequent as the family grew, the water had to be boiled up using the coal boiler in the kitchen of the annex. It was only a small boiler, so the time taken to light and get it up to heat, took hours. The pipe work was unprotected and of large galvanised steel tubing, towering up the inside of the inglenooks chimney, and across into the hot water cylinder next to the bathroom. The coal fired heater was at the far end of the farmhouse, in relationship to the kitchen sink When the hot water was drawn off in the kitchen, the hot water would take ages to come through because of the distance it had to travel.

When we were little we usually had the help of Dad when we had a bath. Just below the sink next to the bath there was a large hole in the floor, allowing a strong draught to come through, making the bathroom very cold in winter. We were made to undress and get into the bath, before the water was cool enough to sit in comfortably. When we got out, dad not knowing his own strength; was not too gentle when drying us off. As we protested against his roughness he reminded us that a good scrub with the towel was good for the skin.

We used to spend a good deal of time rummaging around the items stored near to the water heater in the annexe kitchen. There were the gas masks from the war, and all the worn out old boots and shoes whose leather had become very hard and beyond repair.

Alongside was the shoe iron or last for mending the boots replacing the hobnails, which had become worn after walking on the farmyard cobblestones. When Paul and I were 3 and 4 years old we would select a pair of the hob nailed boots, and a pair of leather gaiters. With the leather gaiters reaching up to our thighs, we would drag the boots enjoying the sound of the studs dragging along the terracotta red clay slate tiles, feeling as big and as important as Dad, leaving a trail of silver lines as we went. It was not long before Mum was on our tale scolding us and getting us to remove the boots, because for her it meant a lot of hard work to remove the marks.

All the bedroom floors were fitted with well polished black painted wood boarding. The floor of the bedroom Paul and I slept in had as much as a 4-inch slope running from the centre of the house to the outside wall. To get the bed level, I had to put at least two thick books under the legs at the foot of the bed. Laying still one night after I had turned the light out, I sensed as if the cover of the pillow was being touched. To begin with I just thought it was me just moving my head slightly, but the sensation appeared to continue. So I turned the light on to see if there was any logical explanation, to notice little black specks of dirt along the back of the pillow, and onto the sheet underneath. I soon realised what they were, for I had seen the same little tell tail signs down in the kitchen cupboard, they were mouse droppings. It then dawned on me what was happening. The mice were regularly coming for a feast having discovered all the crumbs from my sandwiches that I had been eating in bed. The very next morning I set about locating as many mouse traps I could find, polishing the trip wire and catch to make them as sensitive as possible. The next night I positioned three of the traps, loaded with cheese, in strategic places under the bed, and happily went off to sleep. Mum or I had hoovered up all the breadcrumbs, but a few small morsels of cheese were placed close to the traps. It was not long before the snap of one of the traps shutting woke me up. I quickly put the light on and discarded the dead mouse, resetting the trap and getting back to sleep. Every night for the next week or so I spent on safari, catching up to three mice a night. I felt quite proud of my on-slaught.

Mum was very caring and sensitive towards us especially if ever we got upset or felt unwell. If we had toothache, or a cold, and as we were too small to swallow an Aspirin whole, she would crush part of the Aspirin into a powder, mix it with some honey, then we could pallet it easily, without noticing the acid taste. If we had ear ache, she would pour some olive oil into a tea spoon then warm it over a lighted candle. Then gently allowing you to lay the side of your head on her lap, she would gently pour the warm liquid oil in. You would have to lay there for a few moments, while she tore off a piece of cotton wool, rolling it into a ball and gently press it into the ear, to prevent it spilling out onto the pillow case at night.

One late summer evening, we were sharply awakened by Mum, to the smell of burning rags. The electricity was off so no lights were working, so we had to feel our way down to the bottom of the stairs, and told to stay there. To our horror as we got to the bottom of the stairs we could see flickering flames showing through the sides of the closed lounge door. Dad had already been alerted by the smell, and had jumped out of bed, popping his slippers on, aimed for the door in the dark. But, as it was pitch black, had miss-judged the wall, blinding himself in his left eye as he hit the light switch. It was an old type of switch, with a protruding brass peg to switch the light on and off. This was the same eye that was already partially blind, but this incident finished off the sight in the eye completely.

Undeterred he rushed down stairs to realise that the fire was stopping him passing through the living room to the back kitchen entrance to where the fire extinguisher was. Fortunately the fire extinguisher was in the outhouse entrance outside the locked kitchen door, so being able to get out through the front door on the lake side of the house, he than ran round the outside of the house, through the lower part of the farmyard, loosing his slippers on the way, and getting well stung by stinging nettles. Hastily he reached for the fire extinguisher, and made his way back. As he lunged in through the front door, he dropped the top end of the extinguisher onto its knob to set it off. Then gently opening the lounge door a little, he aimed the extinguisher jet into the fire that was localised on a table immediately in front of where he was standing. Mum was still standing at the bottom of the stairs, while Paul and I sat on the stair steps anxiously hoping Dad would be able to extinguish the fire. Thankfully the fire had not taken sufficient hold and the fire was soon put out. When the fire was finally damped down, we discovered on a table was a pile of chard clothes waiting to be ironed, with a burnt out iron bedded underneath. Mum on her way to bed had sub-consciously turned the iron on, thinking she had turned it off, causing the iron to heat up till it had ignited the clothes. Jane was still a baby, yet we still do not know why she was not awakened and brought down stairs, for she was fast asleep right above the fire, while all this activity was going on.

On another occasion in winter Dad got dressed one morning and came down stairs to rekindle the fire as usual, to hear a roaring sound up the chimney, the chimney was on fire. We had experienced the lounge chimney going on fire a number of occasions previous, so he shot off out to fetch the fire extinguisher that was now wisely repositioned on the sidewall at the bottom of the stairs. Again he dropped the top of the extinguisher onto its knob to set it off, letting all the fluid up into the chimney, but the roar continued. There was no alternative but to call the fire brigade. To make a call, you had to dial '0' first, wait for the operator to ask for the number you wanted, and then give them the number you were calling from. Our farm is on the border of two counties, so not all the services come from the same county. At that time the driving and car licences were from Hereford, while the fire service came from Worcester, although the telephone exchange dialling system from Worcestershire ran well inside the Herefordshire boundary. The brigade was very quick arriving, yet it took ten minutes pumping water down the chimney, before there was any sign of the fire starting to abate. Then damp smelly steaming coke like clinkers started to roll down the chimney and fill the grate, taking a number of barrow loads to clear.

Dad religiously kept the chimney swept more than once during the winter season. But this was an old inglenook chimney that had been bricked up into a smaller fireplace. A sheet of asbestos had formed a ceiling at the base of the large chimney, creating a platform above the fireplace, where the soot could settle, outside the reach of the chimney brush. On this occasion the chimney had caught fire sometime during the night before, and was ablaze, eating into the soot above the asbestos ledge.

There were hazards to living on the farm at any time of the year, not least when we had any large downfalls of thunder rain. The fields on the west side of the farm fell steeply towards the farmstead, with the lake being the first place where the water could collect. Along the length of the farmhouse each room from the kitchen through the lounge along the front entrance hall along the annexe kitchen and into the annexe lounge the floors fell away a total of two feet. Outside the house, was a path leading from the kitchen sloping down to the annexe lounge, totally enclosed at the annexe end by a stonewall. At the bottom of the path there was a land drain, but it was only a soak away, so it could not carry any great amount of rainwater. Whenever there was a large thunderstorm all the drains in the farmyard would over flow and the water would head for the drain outside the farmhouse kitchen, immediately diverting down this path. In minutes the drain would cease flowing, so the water would soon creep up over the door of the annexe lounge, ruining the carpet that Mum had put down to keep for visitors. After one violent storm the water came up above the 6" step of the annexe lounge surging through the annex kitchen and through the outside door of the entrance hall, taking a short cut straight into the lake. The carpet and much of the furniture were ruined on this occasion.

Aunty Rosie came to stay with us one late Easter. It was so hot that she and us all got sunburnt. One morning of her stay my aunty and I were stood in the entrance of the front door looking across the orchard over to the other side of the lake when a sharp breeze started to get up. But this was no ordinary kind of breeze for in a few moments it turned into a large whirlwind of at least 15 feet in diameter. In a very few moments it travelled down the slope of the orchard, and by the time it reached the lake it was only 18 ins in diameter but had gained height. On the edge of the lake was a boathouse, and as the whirlwind slipped down into the water it caught the one supporting leg, giving it an almighty judder. But when it reached the water it created a small tornado about 3 feet high, drifting into the lake and then fizzled out. A phenomenon I have never seen repeated, apart from seeing hay lifted into the air and carried into an adjacent field.

One piece of furniture in the annexe lounge that did not get damaged during the floods was grandmother Davies' harmonium organ. Mum allowed me to experiment on my grandmother's organ, finding out how the foot pedals worked and how to press the notes to get a sound or two out. Around the age of three, Dad and Mum took me on one of our infrequent visits to Grandad and Gran Townsend's farm in Hoarwithy. Grandmother Townsend

155

also had a harmonium, and while visiting gave me permission to get out a few disjointed sounds while standing with one foot on the one peddle, and my nose just appearing above the height of the keyboard. When I had finished my serenade, Gran came over to me and remarked, *"That was lovely, you will make a good musician one day"*. In spite of how young I was those few words of encouragement had a profound effect on me.

The organ back at home, which had belonged to Gran Davis before she had passed away, was a great help to me housed in the granny flat at the far end of the farmhouse. In my eleventh year I was again tinkering with the organ keys, while a missionary friend Fred Smith was staying with us. He came into the room and saw me tinkering on the notes, with my mum's 'First Steps in Music' tutor book open on the organ. He simply pointed to the note 'C' on the organ, relating it to the note in the music book, indicating how the scale of notes were spaced on and between the lines, and then left me to fend for myself. I soon started to master the notes, getting to grips with the music that only used white notes and then gingerly started to practice with sharps and flats. Getting to grips with music in sharps was much more difficult. In later years I discovered that the playing of sharps on an organ or any instrument with keys were more difficult than flats, whereas when playing the guitar the opposite was apparent, with the sharps easy and the flats hard to play. Whenever I had to play sharps, I discovered that if I started on a key above or below the correct note to play, I could transpose the music into flats so then I could play the music much easier.

Once I had mastered the tutor book, I started looking through the hymnbooks that we used at the chapel, starting with the simple plain tunes, and then moving up to the more difficult ones. Once Gran Townsend discovered that my playing ability was growing, each Christmas and birthday she would ask me what christian music book I would like to have, for a present, so building up my knowledge of tunes. I soon found I could retain the tunes to memory, and elegantly play by ear.

Because of the social limitations on the farm, and no other forms of recreation, I would recluse to the annexe lounge every spare moment, spending up to three hours at a time practicing. I would be there while waiting for dinner, there again after tea and during the evenings, soaking up the stresses that came my way when Dad got upset and things got difficult on the farm. It did not matter whether it was summer or winter I would enjoy practising. Even during winter, without heat from a fire in the grate, I would still continue to practice, with my hands becoming almost too frozen to play. Yet the rich Christian spiritual enrichment I got from the music and especially the words, more than outweighed the cold. Over the next five years my musical ability rapidly grew. The friends at the Gaines invited me one Sunday to a church in Birmingham. In the afternoon they invited us back to the church to the Covenanters boys Group to discover the leader and organist had not turned up, so Reg affectionately turned to me and asked me if I would be willing to help. I had never played in public before, nor had I ever played on a piano, but I nervously accepted. It was quite uncanny to discover that the resident organist's name was David Townsend.

I had become used to the organ using the foot pedals to increase the sound and the expression pedal that sat to the right of my knee to bring feeling to the tunes, but playing the piano was totally different. The expression was attained by how sharp you touched the keys, producing a louder note, and with the piano you could get the melodies to respond much quicker and brighter bringing more life to the music, much more upbeat than the organ. I grew to love playing the piano, which gave me greater inspiration and a richer Christian joy in my spirit.

I was smitten with the piano and decided I would love to have one, allowing me to develop a wider and deeper richness to the Christian music I had already learnt. So in the fullness of time I was permitted to have a piano, when one became available. The owners of the haulage company who lived next to the chapel offered me a piano. I quickly took their kind offer, but I would have to get it home some how. We decide to take the tractor and trailer the four miles journey to collect it. Joining the driver to collect the piano was a young undergraduate from Birmingham University training to get a degree in music. Once the piano was loaded onto the trailer, he then sat on the piano seat and dutifully played the piano the full journey back along the road to the farm. Once home I could not have it in the annexe lounge along side the organ because there was not the space, so I had to have it in the main living room. I could not enjoy the solitude and freedom I once had, for someone would soon complain of me playing or disturbing them, nor could I feel the spirit of the music in company that were not experiencing the indwelling presence of God's Holy Spirit. Thankfully, Reg and Audrey continued to give me freedom to visit them at any time, so I was able to enjoy playing on their piano in the large conference room. The resonance of the large conference room enhanced the sound of the piano bringing a richer depth to the music.

Chapter 10

Change of Career

When my fifteenth birthday came, I considered the best option was to leave school as soon as possible, and work on the farm. This would ease the fears that had developed in me, I then could have some space to myself, able to escape having people constantly pushing me forwards. I could now find my own lonely way, avoid mixing with society, away from the evils of the world, that had been so impressed on me through childhood, and allow the pleasures of the farm to give me fulfilment, and hide behind the seclusion. In my early days of working on the farm Dad permitted me to take a leading hand with the sheep, especially during the lambing season. Dad dedicated himself to running the dairying, which gave me a level of freedom and independence, and lose myself in amongst the sheep. This was part of God's plan for my life, discovering some of the virtues and characteristics of sheep especially during the lambing season. It gave me much joy, pleasure and satisfaction, and the desire maybe to have some breeding sheep of my own in later years. Through this time I learnt at first hand the beautiful characteristics of the Good Shepherd, and at times the waywardness of His sheep, bringing the bible alive when applying the principles to our own lives.

Although I was regularly paid at the start of the short 18 months I spent actually working on the farm, the payments started to rapidly fall off till I received no wages at all. On receiving my first pay packet, which was an accumulation of a few weeks pay, I decided to take myself off on the bus to Worcester and treat myself. The farms woodwork tools were very satisfactory, but the hand tools for the tractors and machinery were very inadequate, so I decide to spend nearly all my first wages on tools, which I considered very necessary. On getting back home from my spending spree I was looked down upon as having taking a very unwise decision followed by words of criticism receiving no encouragement. I found the tools immensely valuable while working on the farm, and little did my family realise how invaluable those tools would be to me in the future. When I left the farm and for many years to come I serviced and maintained cars for my colleagues, as well as my own. The tools continue to give me very good service as well as giving me a lifetime of pleasure. I could have so easily been misguided by the lack of encouragement by my parents. It may be that the lack of forthcoming wages was a way of controlling my spending, but maybe I shall never know.

As soon as I was seventeen, Dad was very willing to send off to the tax office to get me a driving licence. After all I would then be able to drive the tractors on the road and once I had passed my driving test be able to drive the van on the milk round. In order to get some additional income we were doing some subcontract work on other farms like grass cutting and haymaking, so Dad always had to drive me there and asked the farmer to give him a lift back to the farm. But now if I had my own driving licence I could make an earlier start and go to the various farms under my own steam, while Dad was still milking the cows.

I had not been working on the farm for more than twelve months; when I was surprised to receive a letter from my old metalwork teacher, at the Secondary Modern School in Worcester. On the pretence of bringing me some of his old cast off clothes, which he thought I might be able to use on the farm, he and his wife made a bold request to come and visit me, to discover how I was getting on, to which I gladly accepted. After spending a good part of the afternoon in conversation with them over a cup of tea, they asked me if I would like to visit them in Worcester, to which I nervously said thank you. Before leaving they agreed to write again, to arrange the day for my visit that was convenient to us all. Soon they had to say farewell, as they had to leave in time to catch the bus back to Worcester. As I walked with them out through the front door to accompany them down the path onto the Gaines private drive which led to the main road, Mr. Jones turned to me when out of earshot and with a gracious but emphatic tone said. *"David, this life style you have on the farm is not the best for you, you need to have a career"*. He reminded me of how well I had done at metalwork, and how well I would do in making engineering a career. He asked me to give it some serious consideration, and suggested we discuss the matter again, when I came to visit him.

As I reflected on Mr. Jones' parting words I realised my life had some sort of routine where I felt secure, but here I was being pushed into the unknown world again. If I accepted his suggestion

I would no longer be in charge of myself, as far as being in charge goes. Dad and mum had such an influence and control on my life, hemming me in on every side, and yes what future would that bring me. I felt a sudden loneliness, for I had no one to talk to, and felt terribly nervous about it. Things were moving fast, I felt I could not easily escape, yet deep down I knew I needed some freedom and independence somehow, knowing it would mean a lot of nerve racking changes. I felt so helpless unaware of the love and affection that other parents were giving their children and not having received any form of encouragement. I froze up inside loosing all my confidence, even to go and catch the bus, and to visit them. I was nervously worked up inside hoping I'd get the time right for the visit, and then when I got to Worcester, hope I would not find it too difficult getting to Mr. Jones's house.

I managed to arrange a Saturday afternoon off when I did not need to help with the milking. I found Mr. Jones's home relatively easy, as he had generously given me instructions in his last letter. It took him little time to ask me if I had given any more thought to my career, and soon asked me if I wanted to go ahead with an apprenticeship in engineering. I was aware that it was Saturday afternoon and out of working hours, but once I said 'yes' to starting a new career, he immediately got onto the telephone at the home of the senior apprentice lecturer in one of the local factories, asking if he had a spare place for me. After putting the telephone down, he spent little time in calling for his wife, requesting her to write a letter to the lecturer at the factory on my behalf, stating that I wished to attend for interview, could he please arrange. Moments later she returned with a pen for me to sign the letter, and they did the rest.

Back at the farm it was very unusual for me to ever get any post; so obviously when a letter arrived for me with a company stamp on the top questions were asked. Nervously I had to explain what I had decided to do; yet while they obviously showed some unspoken disapproval, they did not act in any unhealthy way or try to dissuade me.

My interview soon came, and in the fullness of time I had a further letter offering me a job. In spite of being two years older than the rest of the lads in the factory apprentice school I was offered an apprenticeship including one day off each week to attend the local Technical College to gain qualifications. In the first year of travelling to and from work the days were very long, for I had to catch the bus at 7.00am in the morning, by making the same speedy journey down the Gaines driveway on my bicycle, to the main road, as before when I was at school. Then when I reached the bus station in Worcester, I would have to make a dash up the high street, to another bus station to get my connection to the factory which was on the opposite side of town, invariably missing the early connection, getting me to work every day late. Thankfully my long working days on the farm were over, and my weekends freed up, By now my brother Paul had left school so he took over and helped on the farm.

After twelve months in the Apprentice School I was given a placement in the factory. Factory life is a very tough place for a Christian to work in, but an excellent training ground to strengthen your faith and develop your evangelistic ability. Having lived in a very sheltered Christian community, I found it hard; hearing a constant dialog of course foul language, with continuous obscene conversations always within earshot. Getting drunk the previous evening seemed to be their normal pastime, and next day glorying in the suffering of an acute headache that they thought was the norm. As a Christian you immediately clashed with this type of lifestyle, for as soon as you began a conversation, you would create some sarcastic ridicule, when you told them of the way a Christian conducted their life. Saying nothing, keeping sincere and not responding to their type of vulgar humour, that constantly bombarded you, was sufficient to tell them you were different. I soon learnt to my cost that if I tried to defend my Christian beliefs to a group I would be outnumbered by ridicule. When the opportunity arose to witness about my faith, I learnt to talk to them on a one to one basis. You could only talk to them as a group when there was a genuine interest, and they wanted to learn, but graciously close the discussion if someone started to become argumentative.

I soon struck up a good friendship with Phil, one of the other apprentices whom lived at Malvern. We would spend our lunchtimes together, and have the opportunity to share my faith with him. I would take with me copies of the monthly Christian magazine 'Challenge' and distribute them to interested colleagues, Phil included.

After three years into my apprenticeship, I was asked if I would like to work in the library section of the Drawing Office. During this era there was quite a class distinction between the white and blue-collar workers. The canteen was segregated, with one part for worker, who had to collect their meals, whereas the white-collar workers were served. Also for me it meant no more wearing smelly boiler suits, you did not have to clock in, and thankfully I was away from the obscene and vile factory language. So having thought over all these positive good points, I did not take any time to agree to the move.

Living in the Gaines, before Reg and Audrey came were the Lane family. Allan Lane went to the same junior school at Whitbourne. From then on we seemed to follow one another's footsteps, for when I was at school in Worcester he was also in the same class. When I moved into the Drawing Office during my apprenticeship, Allan was again in the same department as I was. One morning a few moments just after I arrived Alan turned to me and said, have you heard about Phil. *"No."* said I. To which he replied *"He's dead"*. I was so shocked. Phil while travelling to work on his motorbike had slipped under an articulated lorry, and was instantly killed. I was thankful I had met Phil and had the opportunity to share my Christian faith with him.

Soon after I left the farm, Dad saw a Ford Poplar E300 van for sale on a local garage forecourt, and to my surprise decided he would purchase it for me. As he had not paid me for some weeks, I decided this vehicle would make up for wages I had not received, so I never did pay Dad anything for it.

One couple at the church who had recently passed their driving tests, and had gained valuable experience of the test route in Hereford, offered to take me each Saturday to Hereford and give me some driving lessons. It was considered better going to Hereford, as it was a rural city, not quite so hustle and bustle, with less traffic to tangle with. Up to this point I had been travelling to work using the bicycle to get to the bus in my usual unorthodox way, having to rise at 6-30am each morning. John Hindle who used to work on the farm, having left the farm to set up his own rented small holding in the village, was now working in another large factory across the street from where I worked. In order to aid his living costs, he volunteered to co-pilot me to work in my own van, saving his petrol, yet furthering me in my driving ability. This meant I could stay in bed for another half hour, enabling me to get to work on time, on most occasions. I soon passed my driving test, at the second attempt.

Now I was working away from the farm, home life did get a little easier, as I began to make new friend from work. As news spread that I was living on the farm, I was able to sell some of the produce, like eggs, potatoes, and spring daffodils. There was a very wise and traditional type of culture among the design team in the Drawing Office who had a great interest in country life. Some were dedicated bird watchers, walkers and conscientious nature lovers so as my relationships grew with them, I was able to invite them out to the farm. In turn I began to visit the various office members' homes, helping them out with practical jobs that required an extra hand. But this caused some jealousy and a build up of tensions back at home with the often said remark, "*You can help everybody else, but you cannot give us an hand*". I felt quite guilty not knowing how to answer and for some years I was not strong enough to defend myself on these issues. But I soon came to realise how that for many years I had been made to work on the farm, in all circumstances, without any kind of encouragement or reward. The practical skills and knowledge I had gained from living on the farm became a great asset in helping others, and above all was much appreciated. The combination of ability and appreciation built a great bond between my colleagues and me.

The sales of farm produce out grew the Ford Cortina car I now owned. I noticed a small 7 cwt trailer belonging to our neighbour rusting in a hedgerow, so I offered him £5 which included a length of angle iron with a ball hitch attached to act as a tow bar. The rear springs on the Ford Cortina soon began to sag badly with use, and quite a high mileage built up on the clock, so with the good wages I was getting, and the small income from the farm, I exchanged it for a Rover 2000. I was now able to take up to ½ ton of potatoes to work at a time, often going in with the trailer Saturday morning for half a day's work, then spend the rest of the afternoon delivering potatoes, getting to know where all the fish and chip shops were in town, to get a much needed mid-day meal.

In the spring Mum would be out in the late afternoons collecting daffodils. Then on Friday which was payday for the workers at the factory, she would be up early morning, to bunch them up with elastic bands, putting them into the buckets of water for me to load into the back of the car.

Later on in the season, just after a very warm sunny period around mid-September, followed by a heavy downpour of warm rain, we would occasionally have a bountiful amount of mushrooms, which were always in demand, and easy to sell.

One season, one of the female members in the office was about to celebrate her 21st birthday, and asked me if I could bring in some flowers, suitable for the occasion. I thought it wise to go in early before I started work to deliver the flowers to her office, to discover that she had a throat infection and lost her voice. As I presented her with the bunch of flowers she started to whisper to me, unable to use her voice. The rest of the office watching the bunch of flowers being exchanged became intrigued not knowing what this young couple were communicating to one another, thinking we were discussing some secret plans the rest of the office were not to know about.

In spite of the effect eczema has on my hand when working in cold water, my heart is still at the farmstead, particular in the area of shepherding. I would like to build a collection of farm machinery of past years, to keep as a memory of our heritage. Both Christina and I would love to have a small holding just to enjoy the memories of days past. We would like the gentle country lifestyle to be a benefit to others needing a retreat, and find that peace and tranquillity, that we all need. Sadly society is leading a very stressful lifestyle, which sadly has become part of today's way of life. This has happened to me, so I have had to retire earlier than I envisage, and maybe these dreams could become a reality quicker than I expected.

Conclusions

Can We Really Say... Lets Get Back to The Good Old Days

People who had a keen interest in farming life would often asked the question. *"Why have you not stayed in farming, living in the beautiful countryside with all the wealth that you will inherit?"* Having lived through the many ups and downs that take place in running a small farming business, coping with the stress and worry, over money and trying to fight the elements, or trying to go along with them, I decided it was better to be small poor and happy, than big complex and entangled with the many worries. If you were to ask friends of mine what sort of a childhood I had while living at the farm, they will jump in my defence and say that I had a very hard and difficult childhood. If I were asked what it was like to live on the farm, I would say that it was very hard work but, a very enjoyable lifestyle, when I had the opportunity to get away from the farmhouse and intermingle with the animals and accompany the farm workers. Christina and myself would both love to return to our roots, and re-live our childhood memories, taking on a small property where we could enjoy our retirement. When you get to know true country people, you will discover very happy and loving people, making and having time to talk and get to know you. They are generous, willing to help and share, but have a wealth of wisdom, shrewd in doing business, wise and resourceful with very strong personalities. Thankfully, still today, on the larger estates, the community spirit is still alive, utilising the wisdom and knowledge that helps to keep country life alive. Frequently, when folk discovered my farming roots, they were often known to comment, *"Do you know how to find a fool in the countryside? You have to take one with you."*

Before I was taken ill, Chris and I spent some months regularly visiting a farm where they took in young men suffering from the results of drug and alcohol abuse. We were there on a pastoral role, teaching them Christian ethics, taking them through a rehab program, to help them come off the drugs and alcohol. These young men were encouraged to work and feed the animals, giving them a lot of joy and fulfilment, and helping them to readjust to the normal ways of life. We often hear of similar farmsteads where children and adults can stay to help those suffering from varying levels of trauma, with good results, with many able to go back to living a normal lifestyle.

There must be a simple answer to why this lifestyle is so attractive and fulfilling. When mankind was first created, he was told that he was to till the ground, and have control over all creeping things on the planet. So the desire to work on the land, to feed and nurture the animals is part of our nature as much as having an appetite to eat. When man was created, some of those in high places in the heavens started a power struggle, with Lucifer (Satan) being thrown out. Ever since then, he is trying to get his own back on mankind by persuading us to become power seekers, and implanting the desire to do wrong instead of right, which we all know is the easiest thing in our nature to do. That power struggle is still as prevalent today, bringing poverty and wars.

If we were to cut out all the modern inventions of mankind, and resort to the lifestyle of the age two hundred years ago, we would again find we were not working to the watch, but able to spend our free time to socialise, revitalising the community spirit. We could engage in our work and social activities, without the noise of modern commerce like aeroplanes, cars and large farm machinery, which are a constant danger and could in an instant, kill us. Modern mechanisation, means fewer workers, bringing isolation and loneliness, with more attempted suicides.

The latest trend is to go to the gym for a workout every day, or go to the weight watchers to keep fit. Getting back to our roots and having the joy of working to produce our own food would cut out all these modern synthetic exercises, giving us better health. Having the privilege of walking out of your house and getting all your produce fresh, would cut out all the health dangers that are tied up in having to keep and store food for days, even weeks, and then developing some degree of contamination, before they get to the table.

We may ask the question, will things ever be the same? Will we see traditional values come back, in a world that has moved so far on in one generation?

[1] It will return, but not in this present age. No longer will you have to keep pulling up the thorns and creepers, which seek to

---

[1] Biblical Prophecy's taken from…Isaiah. Ch 2 verse 4 & Ch 65 verse 25.

strangle other plant life. Children will be able to play outside the den of snakes and not get bitten. Lions and animals of prey will eat grass like the cows. Peace will return to this world, with all the armament and ammunition of war being recycled for ploughs and agricultural work.

I cannot wait for it to happen

Index to photos and illustrations